The United States Supreme Court and Politics

The United States Supreme Court and Politics

Judicial Retirements, the Docket, and the Nomination Process

Justin P. DePlato - with
Matthew M. Markulin

LEXINGTON BOOKS
Lanham • Boulder • New York • London

Published by Lexington Books
An imprint of The Rowman & Littlefield Publishing Group, Inc.
4501 Forbes Boulevard, Suite 200, Lanham, Maryland 20706
www.rowman.com

6 Tinworth Street, London SE11 5AL, United Kingdom

British Library Cataloguing in Publication Information Available

Library of Congress Cataloging-in-Publication Data
Names: DePlato, Justin P., author.
Title: The United States Supreme Court and politics : judicial retirements, the Docket, and the nomination process / Justin P. DePlato.
Description: Lanham : Lexington Books, 2019. | Includes bibliographical references and index. | Summary: "While commonsense attitudes towards the United States Supreme Court have been focused on what decisions they are likely to make, this book focuses on the impacts of other politicized elements of the Court, such as the nomination process, docket selection, and judicial retirements"—Provided by publisher.
Identifiers: LCCN 2019043139 (print) | LCCN 2019043140 (ebook) | ISBN 9781498512183 (cloth) | ISBN 9781498512190 (epub)
Subjects: LCSH: United States. Supreme Court—Officials and employees—Selection and appointment—History. | Judges—Selection and appointment—United States—History.
Classification: LCC KF8742 .D47 2019 (print) | LCC KF8742 (ebook) | DDC 347.73/26—dc23
LC record available at https://lccn.loc.gov/2019043139
LC ebook record available at https://lccn.loc.gov/2019043140

We dedicate this book to the merits of the law. We in the Republic must stress that the law is king, not the Court.

Contents

Acknowledgments

We would like to thank all of the critical reviewers of the book for their helpful insight and suggestions. The review process was fair and helped us form a better book.

Introduction

In American politics today, it is common knowledge that the Supreme Court is a politicized entity, and that its ideology will often affect the decisions it tends to make and the policies and social issues it will likely support. Consider Thurgood Marshall's blunt statement of his own legal philosophy: "You do what you think is right and let the law catch up."[1] Exceptions to partisanship tend to surprise us, as in the case of Chief Justice John Roberts who cast the deciding vote in *National Federation of Independent Business v. Sebelius* when the Roberts Court ruled in favor of the Individual Mandate, a controversial aspect of the Affordable Care Act, much to the chagrin of conservatives who expected otherwise from Roberts. While common-sense attitudes toward the Court have been focused on what decisions they are likely to make, this book aims to focus on other politicized elements concerning the Supreme Court, such as the nomination process and judicial retirements.

The politicization of the Court has always been a legitimate concern regarding an unelected and undemocratic institution; as such, this book reveals important implications of this politicization in a way that relates the institutional implications with social implications. In the last decade, there has been a groundswell of burgeoning social issues; the court has ruled that individuals have the right to keep and bear arms for the purposes of self-defense,[2] that the Affordable Care Act passes constitutional muster,[3] and that the right to marry is guaranteed to same-sex couples by the Constitution.[4] A court that respects ideology more than justice, and one which aims its efforts at political expediency first and its core purposes second poses a great risk to the legitimacy of the Court itself.

MOTIVATION AND IDEOLOGY

While ideology can often reflect the political climate in which the Court exists, there are underlying juridical ideologies which inform jurists on a fundamental level; this is the focus of chapter 1. Consider the legalist and the attitudinal models of juristic thought; both are the product of the long and contentious history of the philosophy of law. As such, there is no consensus on the proper method with which to decide cases presented to the Court. Ideology, on this level, is such that a judge doesn't merely attempt to manipulate the letter and spirit of the law such that it comports with their worldview; rather, the judge's very juridical thinking is informed on the most basic level by this sort of ideology, and, as a result, this ideology contains within it a greater legitimacy and a greater strength than that of more overt, surface-level political ideology. Indeed, it is this lens through which the justice sees legal matters, and it is this lens which has likely shaped them throughout their formative education and early experiences. In other words, it is the way in which they make sense of the world of law, and is more fundamental than circumstantial political goals.

The legalistic and the attitudinal models are the two ideologies explored in chapter 1, and their differences revolve around a basic and contentious question: Is law discovered—or is it created? The legalistic tradition answers this by declaring that the law is discovered and that it pre-exists mankind in the form of rules of reason. The legalistic tradition is the positive correlate of the Natural Law tradition in ethics, whereby certain truths are found out by appealing to reason—a model which is accessible and consistent for any individual with the capacity of reason. To illustrate this basic principle, it is prudent to refer to Montesquieu, who wrote that "Laws, in their most general signification, are the necessary relations arising from the nature of things. In this sense, all beings have their laws; the Deity his laws, the material world its laws, the intelligence superior to man their laws, the beasts their laws, man his laws."[5] However, there are certain subsidiary principles which follow this basic premise of the preexistence of the laws. Emphasis on precedent, original intent, and dispassionate positioning are all features of the legalistic model. Precedent aims to establish the consistency and stability of the law, original intent attempts to retain or uncover the original motivations behind a law or decision, and dispassionate positioning is aimed at disconnecting the jurist's personal beliefs and feelings from the matter at hand—the is what it is, not what the jurist *wants it to be*. These three factors together aim to form a consistent and robust system of law. The law is aimed at justice through consistency and judgement. Reasoning determines the law and arbitrariness and inconsistency are to be avoided and detested.

The attitudinal model entails a great deal more for jurists in the here-and-now. The jurist in this model is an active part of the creation of and administration of the laws; that is to say that judges will have an active role in the shaping and institution of law such that they help aim it toward some good—generally in accordance with their own deeply held principles or those inferred about the good of the political community. It is often held by proponents of this model that law is to respond to the conditions and times in which it finds itself; in this way, it is of the *realist* variety, which posits that we see and accept things simply as they are, rather than pursuing lofty and idealistic goals and theories. The grit of reality, not the clean and pretty theories of the ivory tower, is what is worth consideration. As a result of this, jurists are in the unique position of being able to revise or rescind laws which do not comport with the times in which they find themselves, thereby accessing a direct route to the betterment of a society in accordance with their values or the values of the political community. Judges themselves have to possess the foresight to anticipate social ills or gains that come about as a result of judicial decision-making, or even of the effects that precedent could have. This view is most commonly associated with the idea of an *activist judge*.

POLITICS AS USUAL

The Court operating as a political institution never has been a comforting thought, and aside from individuals who pay it special attention, it is often the case that the politicization of the court is overlooked in virtue of the more obvious and overt politicization of the House, Senate, and presidency. In chapter 2, we argue that the judicial nomination and confirmation process can be affected by factors such as ideological and partisan congruence between the nominee and the Senate, as well as the time during which the nomination takes place.

The ability, therefore, of the presidency and the Senate to influence and shape policy, through their nomination and confirmation of Supreme Court justices, represents an interesting and deservedly controversial mechanic in the workings of American statecraft. It should not require exposition for even a layperson to recognize that this is partisan politics at play once again—not something the American Founders intended of the nomination and confirmation processes. According to our evidence, as it stands now, the confirmation and nomination process is favorable toward liberals, rather than conservatives. This leads to *less* qualified liberals being as likely to be selected as *more* qualified conservatives. Naturally, this impacts the expertise of the court, as individuals are not chosen solely on their ability or qualifications, but rather due to traits which ought to be irrelevant to the duties of a judge. When the

Court is misused for partisan gains, not only does the institution itself suffer, but so does the political community as a whole.

A DIMINISHING DOCKET

Chapter 3 analyzes the issues concerning the number of cases heard by the Court over a specific period of time; the docket size is considered to be an important component of the judiciary because of the effects that it can have on the stability and consistency of law. Thus, when docket sizes become much smaller, because fewer laws are being assessed by the Court, there is less clarity as to the fidelity of the laws with respect to the Constitution. The docket sizes have in fact shrunk rapidly over the course of the last few decades, and it should be concerning when one considers the factors which contribute to this phenomenon.

Like the nomination and confirmation processes, there are both external and internal factors determining the docket size. Many of these are political in nature, unrelated to the juridical duty at hand. These factors include, but are not limited to, how conservative the Court is in general, the number of presidential vetoes issues, and the mean age of the justices on the Court. Interestingly, a more conservative court might be inclined to hear fewer cases due to a rejection of the notion of legislating from the bench, which is often in accordance with principles that tend toward a legalistic model, rather than an attitudinal one.

TILL DEATH DO WE PART

Judicial retirements would seem to be another area ripe for politicization; however, this does not turn out to be the case as often as one might think. It is well known that Justices, given their life-long appointments, often sit on the court for long periods of time—not uncommonly until their death (e.g., Rehnquist and Scalia). Whenever a Justice either passes away or retires, it leaves a vacancy which needs to be filled by the current president. The obvious consequence of this is that the previously discussed biases within the nomination, confirmation, and appointments to the court begin to resurface. This is a chance either for a president to defend their legacy with a like-minded judge, or for a Senate which leans a particular way to do the same with the laws it attempts to pass. It would seem that the timing of retirements, given that can be employed strategically (e.g., waiting to retire under a like-minded president), would be an important factor when considering the politicization of the court.

However, on the contrary, it is often the case that Justices merely retire when they no longer wish to serve on the Court, though, of course, *some* Justices clearly retire due to political and ideological reasons. Given the otherwise politicized state of the Court, it is relieving to see that the retirement process is not routinely abused for ideological gain. Yet, it behooves us to remain somewhat cautious of the fact that it can still, given the opportunity, be exploited. In addition to exploring reasons for retirement in this chapter, we will briefly review the conditions under many recent retirees of Supreme Court justices retired; this analysis goes back several decades. This analysis will provide a way of understanding the degree to which the retirement process is politicized.

A BRIEF CONSIDERATION OF CURRENT KNOWLEDGE

Although one might wish to believe that politics is reserved for the presidency or the legislature, empirical evidence suggests that the Court is politicized and driven by political motivations of many sorts, as we indicated in our brief. The questions that such data prompts us to consider take various forms. For example, what role does politics play on when a justice retires? What role does politics play in determining which cases the Court decides to review? What role does politics play in determining who is nominated to the Bench? We are able, through our analysis, to predict judicial retirements, docket selection, and the likelihood of judicial nominations succeeding. We can further conclude that the Court is very undemocratic and that judicial motivations are increasingly political, rather than merely legal. The universally relevant effect of this political stain on the Court threatens to affect, where it hasn't already outright intervened, civil liberties and social issues in the modern era.

This book, unlike other works, such as Segal and Spaeth (2002), Maltzman, Spriggs, and Wahlbeck (2000), Pritchett (2014), Baum (2012), McCloskey (2010), Murphy (1965), Knight and Epstein (1996), focuses the analysis on institutional factors that are often overlooked; further, the work that would ordinarily be spread across several volumes is succinctly contained in just one; this makes it possible to easily understand the politicization of the Court on the whole.

Much of the scholarly work on the Supreme Court has focused solely on decision- making. Great books were written, such as Segal and Spaeth's tireless work that analyzes the effect of attitude on decision-making (2002); Knight and Epstein's work on understanding the tacit effect of *stare decisis* (precedent) on decision-making is another pertinent example (1996). Other works, such as Pritchett's (2014) study of the Roosevelt era courts, continued the analysis of judicial behavior and looked to understand the political behavior of the justices concerning—primarily—decision-making. One cannot help but mention Murphy's important work on this topic (1965).

The great books written on the history of Court decisions are equally important, such as Baum's (2012) or McCloskey's (2010) works. This book departs from these approaches of either studying decision-making or court decisions exclusively. Instead, this book addresses the institutional factors of the Court's politicization, in their totality, in one volume.

We examine three key areas that are often overlooked: the judicial docket, the judicial selection process, and judicial retirements. In each instance, because the Court is political, the timing of retirement matters, the selection of cases matters, and the nomination of future judges matter when considering politicization on the whole. One could then predict, with this understanding, which retirements are likely or unlikely to occur; one could also predict how cases will be selected by the Court depending on the average political leaning of the Court.

These institutional factors are important to examine because, to an extent, the behavior of justices can be anticipated based on the political circumstances they are present in and that they partially constitute. For example, why did Justice O'Connor wait so long to retire? Was it her ideology dictating the terms of her retirement, or merely an unrelated personal choice? As justices retire, the ideological composition of the Court changes, which means the way in which the Court decides cases will change. Liberal judges know that President Trump will replace them with more conservative judges, and so they are much more likely to forestall retirement if they can. Hence, the composition of the Court is just one important fact about the Court to consider as the country faces burgeoning social issues. The future of the United States is, rightly or wrongly, often predicated on who the next judge will be and what that judge believes and thinks.

The evidence provided in this book draws the strong conclusion that the Court is very political. The Court is an undemocratic, unelected institution that is, at times, more political than the necessarily political branches of government. The argument that the Court is not political is bunk and our analysis proves that the Court's ideological behavior goes much further than simply decision-making. Indeed, the Roberts Court is choosing cases that favor a conservative outcome.

FOR THE READER

We will see, given the evidence presented herein, that the Court is indeed a very political institution; through statistical modeling and other quantitative analyses, this book will present a convincing case as to the depth and extent of the Court's politicization. This account will be appreciable by scholars and, at the same time, be accessible to a layman reader. It is intended to convey the meaning of the politicized Court in a plain, but substantial way. Given this evidence, it is reasonable for a reader to approach the Court in a more skeptical light than they may have previously. Through this cautious skepticism endeavor, the reader is encouraged to uncover for themselves where the truth may lie underneath the politicized decisions of a politicized Court.

NOTES

1. Savage (2010).
2. See *District of Columbia v. Heller*, 554 U.S. 570 (2008).
3. See *King v. Burwell*, 576 U.S. ___ (2015).
4. See *Obergefell v. Hodges*, 576 U.S. ___ (2015).
5. *The Spirit of the Laws*, I.I.

BIBLIOGRAPHY

Baum, Lawrence. *The Supreme Court.* 11th ed. Washington, DC: CQ Press, 2012.

Knight, Jack, and Lee Epstein. "The Norm of Stare Decisis." *American Journal of Political Science* 40, 4 (November 1996): 1018–35.

Maltzman, Forrest, James F. Spriggs, and Paul J. Wahlbeck. "Strategy and Judicial Choice: New Institutionalist Approaches to Supreme Court Decision-Making." In *Approaches, Supreme Court Decision-Making: New Institutionalist*, edited by Cornell W. Clayton and Howard Gillman, 43–64. Chicago: University of Chicago Press, 1999.

———. *Crafting Law on the Supreme Court: The Collegial Game*, 1st ed. Cambridge: Cambridge University Press, 2000.

McCloskey, Robert G. *The American Supreme Court*, 5th ed. Edited by Sanford Levinson. Chicago: University of Chicago Press, 2010.

Murphey, Walter F. "Deeds under a Doctrine: Civil Liberties in the 1963 Term." *The American Political Science Review* 59, 1 (March 1965): 64–79.

Pritchett, C. Herman. *The Roosevelt Court: A Study in Judicial Politics and Values, 1937–1947.* New Orleans: Quid Pro, LLC, 2014.

Savage, Charlie. "Kagan's Link to Marshall Cuts 2 Ways." *The New York Times.* May 12, 2010. http://www.nytimes.com/2010/05/13/us/politics/13marshall.html?pagewanted=all&_r=0.

Segal, Jeffrey A., and Harold J. Spaeth. "If a Supreme Court Vacancy Occurs, Will the Senate Confirm A Reagan Nominee?"*Judicature*, 1986.

———. *The Supreme Court and the Attitudinal Model Revisited.* Cambridge: Cambridge University Press, 2002.

Spriggs, James F., Forrest Maltzman, and Paul J. Wahlbeck. "Bargaining on the U.S. Supreme Court: Justices' Responses to Majority Opinion Drafts." *The Journal of Politics* 61, 2 (May 1999): 485–506.

Wahlbeck, Paul J., James F. Spriggs, and Forrest Maltzman. "Marshalling the Court: Bargaining and Accommodation on the United States Supreme Court." *American Journal of Political Science* 42, 1 (January 1998): 294–315.

Wahlbeck, Paul J., James F. Spriggs, and Forrest Maltzman. "The Politics of Dissents and Concurrences on the U.S. Supreme Court." *American Politics Research* 27, 4 (1999): 488–514.

ADDITIONAL AND RECOMMENDED RESOURCES

Spriggs, James F., Forrest Maltzman, and Paul J. Wahlbeck."Bargaining on the U.S. Supreme Court: Justices' Responses to Majority Opinion Drafts." *The Journal of Politics* 61, 2 (1999): 485–506. http://www.jstor.org/stable/2647513.

Forrest Maltzman, James F. Spriggs, and Paul J. Wahlbeck. "Strategy and Judicial Choice: New Institutionalist Approaches to Supreme Court Decision-Making." In *Approaches, Supreme Court Decision-Making: New Institutionalist*, edited by Cornell W. Clayton and Howard Gillman, 43–64. Chicago: University of Chicago Press, 1999.

Wahlbeck, Paul J., James F. Spriggs, and Forrest Maltzman. "Marshalling the Court: Bargaining and Accommodation on the United States Supreme Court." *American Journal of Political Science* 42, 1 (1998): 294–315. http://www.jstor.org/stable/2991757.

Wahlbeck, Paul J., James F. Spriggs, and Forrest Maltzman. "The Politics of Dissents and Concurrences on the U.S. Supreme Court." *American Politics Research* 27, 4 (1999): 488–514.

Chapter 1

The Court, Ideology, and Decision-Making

The analysis in this chapter presents the contemporary scholarly debate concerning the effects of ideology on judicial decision-making. While the primary focus of this book is the effects of political ideology on the Court concerning institutional factors (e.g., the selection process, docket selection, and retirement), ignoring the contemporary debate over the effects of ideology on decision-making would be an injustice to the reader.

There are two distinct, competing models in political science regarding the way in which a Justice of the Court decides a case: the *Legalist* model and the *Attitudinal* model. These models differ considerably in terms of how a judge ought to reason and decide cases. For instance, one might assume that a judge's task is as simple as, in each case, comparing a petitioner's claim with the law in order to see where they comport and where they diverge, moving to decide the case on that basis. Is the petitioner's claim well-grounded in the plain meaning of the law as it is written? If so, then the case is decided as such. The aforementioned is the basic reasoning of the Legalist model.

However, what if a judge does not like the reasoning that the law brings them to and the decision irritates their particular biases, prejudices, or ideology? Then, accordingly, the judge interprets the law through the lens of their biases to construct an argument that fits nicely into the judge's ideology, arguably a nonlegal conclusion. Scholars disagree about how judges ought to make decisions. Does a judge simply apply the law as best as they can, regardless of their own personal feelings? Or does a judge determine the law and the placement of law with respect to their ideology? Consider the merits and demerits of each model.

THE LEGALIST MODEL

Students of constitutional law know that understanding all of the clauses of the Constitution can be a bit tricky at times. This is often due to debate or ambiguous intent regarding some of the more "flexible" clauses. For instance, what constitutes a "reasonable search" or a "probable cause"? What counts as "cruel and unusual" punishment, as opposed to usual and humane? Due to this ambiguity, judges, when confronted with an injury related to either the Fourth or Eighth Amendment to the Constitution, often have a very difficult task before them insofar as they must determine what the answer, constitutionally, really is. The Legalist model strives to avoid bringing any personal biases or prejudices into the meaning of the law; moreover, it does not attempt to modify the meaning of the law to suit any particular end, whether personal, or for the betterment of society in accord with some other philosophy. Rather, the judge is to weigh the complaint and injury with the essence—that is, the meaning and spirit—of the law and then determine the case.

Legalists are defenders of jurisprudence, and legal reasoning is untainted by human emotion, empathy, and ideology. To understand this logic, one ought to consider Williams Blackstone, a very important English jurist in the 16th century, of whom most students at any prestigious law school will learn. One of the most important Blackstonian conclusions was this simple statement, "The law is discovered . . . [and] . . . judges are the depositories of the laws." He further commented that judges

> are to determine, not according to [their] own private judgment, but according to the known laws and customs of the land; not delegated to pronounce a new law, but to maintain and expound the old one. Yet this rule admits of exception, where the former determination is most evidently contrary to reason; much more if it be clearly contrary to the divine law. But even in such cases the subsequent judges do not pretend to make a new law, but to vindicate the old one from misrepresentation. For if it be found that the former decision is manifestly absurd or unjust, it is declared, not that such a sentence was bad law, but that it was not law.[1]

For the Legalist thinker, the truth of law is discovered, not created, not fabricated, and certainly not manipulated. Consider laws that pre-exist mankind; physicists do not create the laws of physics but rather discover or uncover them. Likewise, Natural Law theorists do not create moral laws; they discover or uncover them. Mankind's job, therefore, according to the Legalist thinker, is simply to discover those great truths and laws that already exist. The latter portion of what Blackstone said in the above quote, however, is precisely what, as we will see, an Attitudinalist thinker would cite as a reason for opposing unjust laws. One key area of difference is that Legalists have a very narrow scope within which they are apt to admit of exceptions, whereas

Attitudinalists, by contrast, have a much wider scope in which they are likely to admit of exceptions.

The Legalist model spans the ages from the expository jurisprudence in the Renaissance to the twenty-first century. What typically connects all Legalist thinkers is that the decisions of the Court are very much influenced by facts of the case in light of the plain meaning of statutes and the Constitution, as well as the prevailing force and magnitude of precedent. To varying degrees, students of the law, professors of the law, jurists, lawyers, legal scholars, and political scientists propound variants of the Legalist model.

Likewise, there are many judges throughout the history of the Court who have supported or subscribed to the Legalist model. Chief Justice Marshall in almost every opinion he ever offered supported the Legalist model in that he thoroughly emphasized the importance of precedent and the plain meaning of the clauses of the Constitution. More recently, Justice Scalia, Justice Thomas, Chief Justice Roberts, Justice Gorsuch, and Justice Alito overtly emphasize the importance of judges abstaining from ideological bias, supporting precedent, and resist legislating from the bench. In lower courts, such as the D.C. Court of Appeals, we find judges like Judge Harry Edwards and Judge Wald who state, "It is the law—and not the personal politics of individual judges—that controls judicial decision making in most cases resolved by this court"; further, "there is little time or inclination to infuse the decision making process with personal ideology" (Edwards 1985; Wald 1999). Yet, despite the claims of these Justices, many have criticized them for doing the opposite of what they advocate. Further, this approach could be considered to be a sort of ideology in its own right.

Precedent is one of the guiding forces for the Legalist thinker. It constrains a judge, forcing them to abandon their own ideology in favor of blind justice. The judge is confined to a narrow space, or a gap that might exist in the law, and the filler is not to be the judge's own ideology. Rather, the gap is filled by finding the union between the case facts, preceding decisions, or the Natural Law. When a case falls clearly within the scope of a previous decision, the earlier case has an "enactment force" that binds the judge. The Legalist judge appreciates the force of precedent, even in cases in which the application of precedent may prove uncomfortable to the judge personally. Justice Hugo Black was another ardent defender of the legalist approach:

> In interpreting the Constitution, Justice Black followed the plain meaning of the words and the intents of the framers. Black, with a near religious fervor for most of his tenure on the Court, fought and argued to base his and the Court's constitutional interpretation on the literal text itself. . . . Always at war against judicial roaming in the murky natural law ether of substantive rights. . . . Black tried to interpret constitutional phrases in accordance with the intent of the Framers and the history of the clause or the Amendment. (Ball and Cooper 1992, 318–19)

Legalist thinkers fervently uphold the doctrine of "plain meaning." Plain meaning applies not only to the language of statutes and constitutional provisions but also to the words of judicially formulated rules. The plain meaning doctrine simply asserts that judges rest their decisions, in significant part, on the plain meaning of the pertinent language. For example, if Article I, section 10, of the Constitution declares that no state shall pass any law impairing the obligation of contract, then the Court should consistently strike down laws that would do so.

American Legalist thinkers also adhere to the intents of the American Framers. Framers' intent refers to construing statutes and the Constitution according to the works of those men who originally drafted and supported the clauses of the Constitution. Significant contributors to the drafting of the original Constitution included, but were not limited to, James Madison, Edmund Randolph, Benjamin Franklin, and Alexander Hamilton. The Justice who adheres to an *Originalist* approach to interpreting the Constitution is trying, by examining primary source documents, to construe from those documents what the intent behind the meaning of a constitutional clause was when the clause was originally written. For example, the First Amendment says Americans have "freedom of speech"—does this clause mean *absolute* freedom, or is this freedom consistent with certain limitations on such speech (as the Court has concluded)? The Originalist would obtain documents from the founding of the nation, as well as historical, scholarly assessments of the founding period and the constitution, which would indicate what the intent and meaning were of the clause at its inception to then determine the answer to the previous question. A good example of this practice in action is the *DC v. Heller* case; reading this opinion gives one a good sense of what Originalism is. Some justices, such as Antonin Scalia, take the plain meaning of the words of the original documents, rather than their intentions, to be what is of primary importance to an Originalist.[2]

Robert Bork, an argent defender of the Framers' intents when interpreting the law, articulates Originalism well, stating,

> The Court's power is legitimate only if it has, and can demonstrate in reasoned opinions that it has, a valid theory, derived from the Constitution, of the respective spheres of majority and minority freedom. If it does not have such a theory but merely imposes its own values, or worse if it pretends to have a theory but actually follows its own predilections, the Court violates the postulates of the Madisonian model that alone justifies power. It then necessarily abets the tyranny either of the majority or of the minority. (Bork 1971, 3)

Bork's conclusions indicate that a strong adherence to Originalism necessitates that the Court "stick close to the text and history of the Constitution, and their fair implications and not construct new rights" (Bork 1971, 8). Justice Hugo Black was another practitioner of the Originalist approach; Black argued often and consistently that intent mattered, especially to protect the rights outlined and enumerated in the Constitution. Of course, ultimately it was the Founders themselves who were being modeled: Madison and Jefferson also favored the importance of intent guiding interpretation, Madison wrote, "if the sense in which the Constitution was accepted and ratified by the Nation . . . be not the guide in expounding it, there can be no security for a consistent and stable government"; Jefferson agreed, "our peculiar security is in the possession of a written constitution. Let us not make it a blank paper by construction" (Goldford 2005, 9). However, it can often be difficult to interpret the Constitution through the intents of the Founders, because not all Constitutional issues or their applications have a robust original literature from which to draw. Regardless, an Originalist does the best job they can to understand and interpret the Constitution the same way a Framer of the Constitution would.

PRECEDENT

Those jurists who support a Legalist model will often cite the principle of precedent as one of the major constraints on, and factors in, judicial decision-making. Precedent, or the Latin *stare decisis*, simply means adherence to what has already been decided. Through precedent, the decisions of today are linked with those handed down over time and the law thereby develops a quality of organic connectedness, as well as creates a strong appearance of stability. Imagine a legal system whereby laws were overturned on a regular basis. There would be no consistency, and the validity of the laws would be void; there would be no basis for legitimacy and respect; clearly, legal stability is critical for maintaining the legitimacy of the law and maintaining a stable, civil society. Legalist jurists correctly understand that they must find ways to connect the case they are hearing with the current law, rather than impose their own prejudice or disposition into the law; often, these personal prejudices and/or predispositions result in either invalidating the law or rewriting it. Judges that adhere to precedent are, therefore, to be highly valued. Instead of invoking their personal passions or ideological biases to determine the correct course of action, they look to past rulings. These jurists write substantive, rich legal opinions that provide a historical review of the Court's prior decisions and then they apply the current case to the laundry list of relevant cases, thereby fitting the law into the appropriate place and meaning inside the scope of current law.

A modern example of a judge faithfully adhering to precedent despite personal differences is Chief Justice Roberts. In the Affordable Care Act Case (*National Federation of Independent Business v. Sebelius* 2011), Chief Justice Roberts diligently and correctly reviewed mountains of cases to map out the legal reasoning supporting the constitutionality of the Affordable Care Act. In so doing, Roberts clearly demonstrates a model of opinion writing that is boldly refreshing and strictly reasoned. This decision was a perfect example of a jurist leaving aside prejudice, bias, and emotion out of the law; he performed his duty; he declared what the law means, and did so in an objective fashion.

Precedent is the very glue by which our legal and judicial systems are upheld and maintained. The application of precedent is vitally important to a viable and appropriate construction of law and constitutional interpretation. The members of the Court have always unanimously held the following to be the truth of the law:

> Adherence to precedent is, in the usual case, a cardinal and guiding principle of adjudication, and considerations of *stare decisis* have special force in the area of statutory interpretation, for here, unlike in the context of constitutional interpretation, the legislative power is implicated, and Congress remains free to alter what we have done. (*California v. Federal Regulatory Commission* 1990)

There are nuances in applying precedent that do not violate the doctrine of adherence to the letter. For example *Obiter Dicta*, or simply *dicta*, is a fancy way of explaining that specified portions of a previous opinion consist of surplus language. Therefore, the judge may restrain or throw out the surplus language because the language is unnecessary without overturning precedent. Moreover, courts may wish to employ a "distinguishing a precedent" method, whereby the court is merely asserting that the facts in the current case sufficiently differ from the situational aspects of the precedent case. There is also a method of "limiting a precedent of principle," whereby a court is merely refining the precedent, or better put, *clarifying* the nature of the precedent. For example, the Court held in *Roe v. Wade*, that a woman has a constitutional right of privacy applicable to reproduction thereby granting a legal protection for women to have abortions in the first trimester. Of course since the 1973 ruling, many alterations to the merits of the law were established, but none of them have squashed the principle of the original precedent (*Maher v. Roe* 1977).

In Table 1.1, 1953–2010 we can see just how often the Court overturns precedent.

The findings in Table 1.1 indicate that the Court is not in the business of overturning precedent. In fact, the Court rarely overturns a prior decision. Further, if we parsed the data to include constitutional cases, those cases with

Table 1.1 Overturning Precedent on the US Supreme Court

Court	*Number of Cases Overturned*	*Overrulings per Term*
Warren	43	2.7
Burger	46	2.6
Rehnquist	39	2.6
Roberts	32	1.9

specific civil liberty injury, or structural power cases, then we notice that the super majority of the cases overturning precedent apply to constitutional questions. Of the four courts mentioned in Table 1.1, a substantial majority of the cases that overturned precedent were cases dealing with constitutional questions.

ATTITUDINAL MODEL

We now move to the second and juxtaposed model of decision-making: the Attitudinal model. This model, unlike the Legalist model, holds that decision-making is to be governed by judicial attitudes, mores, and beliefs. This model of decision-making rebukes openly the naivety of the Legalist model and asserts that the Legalist model simply does not comport with or apply to the reality we experience every day.

The Attitudinal model blends together legal realism, political science, psychology, and economics. The model holds that the Supreme Court Justices decide cases by viewing the facts of the case through their own personal lens. Therefore, if a judge is right or left of center, their ideological backgrounds will drive their decision. For instance, Justice Alito and Thomas vote consistently conservative in cases because they are conservative-minded people; Justices Ginsburg and Breyer vote consistently liberal in cases because they are liberal-minded people. The model clearly reduces the nuances and complex subtleties of judicial decision-making to one simple variable: predisposition. Unlike the Legalist model, which heralds that the law is discovered, and is fervently upheld and more static, the Attitudinalist asserts that the law is very much so created. Jurists are creative people who are legally minded, legally gifted, and very intelligent, and they still possess their own set of beliefs and mores which they bring into the law and onto the bench. It can sometimes be the case for jurists to proclaim to be of the Legalist tract, but practice such a belief attitudinally.

Legal scholar Jerome Frank, one of the earliest legal realists, summarizes nicely the attitudinal skepticism about the legalist model of judicial decision-making

> the truth of the matter over the lack of legal precision is that the popular notion of the possibilities of legal exactness is based upon misconception. The law always has been, is now, and will ever continue to be, largely vague and variable. And how could this be otherwise? The law deals with human relations in their most complicated aspects. The whole confused, shifting helter-skelter of life parades before it- more confused than ever, in our kaleidoscope age. . . . Even in a relatively static society, men have never been able to construct a comprehensive, eternalized set of rules anticipating all possible legal disputes and settling them in advance. Even in such a social order no one can foresee all the future permutations and combinations of events; situations are abound to occur which were never contemplated when the original rules were made. How much less is such a frozen legal system possible in modern times. . . . Our society would be straight-jacketed were not the courts, with the able assistance of lawyers, constantly overhauling the law and adapting it to the realities of ever changing social, industrial and political considerations. (Frank 1949, 5–7)

To continue with Frank's analysis, judges "overhaul" and "adapt" the law. If we hold this assertion, as the Attitudinal model purports, then judges are, in some sense law makers—or at least something very close to law makers (law revisers?). Therefore we must be concerned about what values they have and how they intend to influence and change the law in accordance with those values. Note that we do not mean *solely* their own *personal* interests—those concerning their own wealth, power, etc.—but more broadly their private worldview: their views about the psychology of human begins, which economic systems are best, what is ethical, etc.

One of the valuable things the Attitudinalist supporter has advanced regarding decision-making is the use of spatial modeling and rational choice arguments to predict a judge's decision before the decision is rendered. A very simple way to see this approach at work is to examine a simple spatial model across a legal path of inquiry. As an example, let's say there is a case where the Court is hearing an inquiry into the violation of the Fourth Amendment's probable cause and reasonable search clause. The facts of the case make it difficult to determine if the evidence that was discovered is admissible in court. The evidence was not in plain sight, generally speaking, but given what was necessary to obtain the suspect, whom a warrant called for, the evidence would have been readily available to officers in the normal line of duty. Therefore, the question the Court is confronted with is in respect to intrusiveness. Did the police overextend their boundaries of search and thereby intrude the suspect's house and find inadmissible evidence, or was their search admissible because warrant allowed the intrusion and the object was within the scope of the reasonable search?

Now, the judges must answer the question, but how do they? Let's consider then the following spatial model:

In the spatial model above, there are three judges who will decide this case. In order to decide the case, the judges have two cases to assist them, both are relevant precedent, but their outcomes are slightly different. One supports admission of the evidence, the other does not for different, but legally sound, reasons. The judges, thereby, must decide which precedence they will adhere to and how they will decide the case. Judge 1 favors very little intrusion and sides with case B, because he holds a conservative reading of the Fourth Amendment, which he feels narrowly defines reasonable searches. Judge 3 holds the completely opposite view, whereby, he argues, that the Fourth Amendment allows for expansive but still reasonable searches and probable cause; therefore he supports case B because that case is closer to his reading and views on the Fourth Amendment. The two judges couldn't be more apart on this matter. Luckily, because of a linear function, and the odd number of judges, there is always at least one judge in the middle of the extremities; thereby creating a swing vote or a deciding vote. In this matter Judge 2 is the median position, so his legal reasoning is most important and in this matter his legal reasoning or preferences put him closer to Case A, so that is the final decision of the Court. The point of this spatial model is to elucidate how judges fit into a political linear function and that their behavior is often congruent with their ideological preferences.

Two major assumptions the Attitudinalists make about judicial behavior is that because judges serve for life and have nearly full discretion over their docket, these two rules enable a judge to pursue whatever ends, or decisions they think suits their political or ideological tendencies. There is validity behind these assumptions, however, both rules do not simply mean a judge pursues a decision based on ideology, rather a judge could just as simply adhere to precedent or some other means for deciding the case, in place of ideology. It is worth considering, because judges serve for life and control their docket, whether the Court should continue to be an un-elected institution given the potential for judicial activism.

The Attitudinal approach also advances the methodological proclivities of a rational choice model. The rational choice model paradigm attempts to apply and adapt the theories and methods of economics to the entire range of human political and social practices. Rational choice models are always established on assumptions. Like any model (even statistical modeling is established by assumptions, for example the theory of random sampling), the rational choice model rests on certain assumptions; those include:

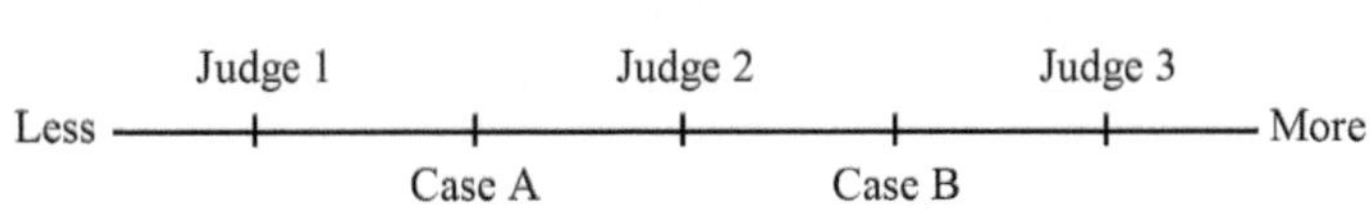

Figure 1.1 *Source:* Author compiled using the Supreme Court Compendium.

1. Actors are able to order their alternative goals, values, tastes, and strategies. This means that the relation of preference and indifference among the alternatives is transitive.
2. Actors choose from available alternatives so as to maximize their satisfaction.[3]

The first statement requires that individuals can rank alternatives such that an individual can determine which outcome they prefer and then pursue it. Justices may want to pursue overturning a case or upholding a case, but first they must determine what their stake and interest is in the issue and where their own dispositions lay in respect to the issue. The second statement requires only that the actor attempt to maximize satisfaction. Actors are allowed to make errors that may or may not frustrate their goals simply because they lack complete information. Recall that in all models incomplete information is the constraint on the quality of the models performance in predicting outcomes. Statisticians like to suggest that their models are superior because as they say "numbers do not lie," however, they covet critical information about the inherent flaws in their models. For example, the assumption of random distribution or sampling, the failure to explain all cases, or to say the cases they do explain are more valuable than the ones they do not, or to not mention to you that in their sample there is at least 5 percent random noise or error, that then is exacerbated in the model resulting in an outcome that is not simply 5 percent wrong, but more likely 10 percent wrong. Of course they dismiss their error by simply asserting that nothing is perfect.

What is beneficial about the rational choice model approach is that the scientist is acknowledging their assumptions, then accounting for them in their tests, and then correctly asserting that the actors have prejudice and bias. Try your luck getting a statistician to admit they have bias and that they mine data. Further, because decision-making really fits into a linear function, the result of the game is a true equilibrium, at least in the meaning of an observation. We never really know what the mind of judge is thinking, we only know what their output is or their decision is, they may still dislike the decision, but we will never know that. The following deduction then is very simple: the actors will compete to win along the linear function, whereby the median position then is the most valuable or powerful position. The outcome will always tend closer to the median than the extremity. Now, of course the median position will move and at one point in time be more right of center and then more left of center, but what remains true is that the median position is driving the behavior the Court and the decision results from the median position pressure.

In light of this, if the attitudinal model is adopted, or is held to be the correct model of jurisprudence, then the role of political science expands to encompass the study of the effects of the attitudes of judges on society. Moreover, perhaps an additional role afforded to the political scientist should be that they offer some counsel, based on their research, as to which judge is likely to produce the greatest benefits in society. Since judges are affected by their ideology, as a consequence, predicting their behavior before it happens would become the job of the political scientist.

NOTES

1. William Blackstone, as quoted in McGinnis and Rappaport (2013, 159).

2. Scalia offered this definition of his own position: "The theory of originalism treats a constitution like a statute, and gives it the meaning that its words were understood to bear at the time they were promulgated. You will sometimes hear it described as the theory of original intent. You will never hear me refer to original intent, because as I say I am first of all a Textualist, and secondly an Originalist. If you are a Textualist, you don't care about the intent, and I don't care if the framers of the Constitution had some secret meaning in mind when they adopted its words. I take the words as they were promulgated to the people of the United States, and what is the fairly understood meaning of those words" (Scalia 1996). Scalia is an example of an Originalist who doesn't adhere, necessarily, to the original intent. Samuel Alito has been referred to as "Scalito" for adhering to a conservative judicial philosophy that is very similar to Justice Scalia (Sekulow n.d., see footnote 77).

3. See Riker (1990).

BIBLIOGRAPHY

Ball, Howard, and Phillip J. Cooper. *Of Power and Right: Hugo Black, William O. Douglas, and America's Constitutional Revolution.* 1st ed. Oxford: Oxford University Press, 1992.

Bork, Robert H. "Neutral Principles and Some First Amendment Problems." *Indiana Law Journal* 47, 1 (1971): 1–35. http://digitalcommons.law.yale.edu/cgi/viewcontent.cgi?article=4149&context=fss_papers.

California v. *Federal Regulatory Commission.* 495 U.S. 490, 499 (1990).

Edwards, Harry T. "Public Misperceptions Concerning the Politics of Judging: Dispelling Some Myths about the D.C. Circuit." *University of Colorado Law Review* 56 (1985): 619.

Frank, Jerome. *Law and the Modern Mind.* New York: Coward and McGann, 1949.

Goldford, Dennis J. *The American Constitution and the Debate over Originalism.* Cambridge: Cambridge University Press, 2005. See footnote 24 for Madison's quote.

Maher v. Roe. 432 U.S. 464 (1977). See other reproduction rights cases.

McGinnis, John O., and Michael B. Rappaport. *Originalism and the Good Constitution.* Cambridge, MA: Harvard University Press, 2013.

Riker, William H. "Political Science and Rational Choice." In *Perspectives on Positive Political Economy*, edited by James E. Alt and Kenneth A. Shepsle, 163–81. Cambridge: Cambridge University Press, 1990.

Scalia, Antonin. "A Theory of Constitutional Interpretation." In *Remarks at the Catholic University of America*. Washington, DC, October 18, 1996.

Sekulow, Jay. "The Judicial Philosophy of Supreme Court Nominee, Samuel Alito." *American Center for Law and Justice*. n.d.

Wald, Patricia M. "A Response to Tiller and Cross." *Columbia Law Review* 99, 1 (January 1999): 235–61. http://www.jstor.org/stable/1123601.

Chapter 2

Judicial Nominations and Ideology

SOME COMMENTS ON THE LITERATURE

Judicial nominations to the Supreme Court of the United States are not simple affairs. Often, the process is muddied with contention, drama, and tabloid speculation. Over the past 25–35 years, the process has unequivocally become more contentious, scrutinized, and important to senators; senators increasingly desire to sit on the judiciary committee and view the assignment to such a committee as prestigious. Such observations suggest that the judicial nomination and confirmation process has become more important to senators.

Several thorough analyses have been conducted to examine the nature and impetus of the burgeoning politicization of the judicial nomination process. With very little doubt, the analyses of presidential appointments and Senate confirmations are both extensive and exhaustive (Abraham 1974; Cole 1934; Danelski 1964; Epstein and Segal 2007; Friedman 1983; Grossman and Wasby 1972; Halper 1972; Haynes 1960; Schmidhauser 1979; Scigliano 1971).

The traditional method employed to explore the confirmation process has been a case-by-case study examining the factors contributing either to the confirmation or the defeat of a nominee (Abraham 1974; McHargue 1949). While this technique offers an examination of empirical data, it is *too* focused on case-by-case studies; unfortunately, this limits the ability of scholars to present broad explanations and theories explaining the confirmation process—though critical theoretical suppositions are sometimes found in such methods. For example, Warren assessed the process in political terms, understanding most judicial rejections were part of a partisan assault. In fact, he claimed that the strongest opposition occurred when the president and the majority party were of opposite party. This phenomenon is even greater during the president's final year in office. In addition, Warren observed the effect of a nominee's politics causing Senate opposition along with senatorial courtesy[1] causing a few nominations to fail (Warren 1922).

McHargue (1949) is also responsible for our understanding of the judicial nomination process. In particular, he found partisan politics to be a major criterion in confirmation battles; claiming they accounted for roughly 10 of 21 rejections (McHargue 1949). Furthermore, his findings validated Warren's earlier findings about the political stances of the nominees having an impact on the process, as did the remainder of the president's tenure and their political party (Warren 1922). Abraham (1974) found similar effects for explaining judicial rejections; he found Senate opposition to the president to be one of the most prominent reasons for rejection. In addition, he validated the lame duck effect[2] and the nominee's politics as reasons for opposition.

Scigliano, using more advanced methods, found that partisan control of the Senate, the timing of the nomination, and the potential for senatorial courtesy all affected the likelihood of confirmation. Scigliano's (1971) analysis confirmed that the timing of the nomination in relation to the president's term to be critical, along with the partisan composition of the Senate in relation to the president's party.

While it is clear that there is abundant research on the topic of judicial nominations and the resulting confirmation or rejection, the key factor that explains the outcome remains unclear. Scholars have long hinted at the fact that ideology is a critical factor in terms of explaining the outcome, yet there is little analysis that can conclude ideology is a determinate variable which is statistically worthwhile. In 2009, former Speaker of the House Newt Gingrich stated in an interview with Greta Van Susteren that "it's more difficult to get a conservative approved than it is to get a liberal" (2009). Yet, can we as scholars definitively confirm or disconfirm the former Speaker's claim? In order to do so we offer a logit time analysis to capture the change in the number of days from appointment until confirmation or rejection, with the goal of explaining whether or not ideology is truly a critical factor in the confirmation process.

As indicated in Table 2.1, by utilizing a simple means test to compare 17 conservative (Red), 11 liberal (Blue), and 2 neutral (Pale) (see Figure 2.1) candidates for judicial nominations, the average wait time found was 46 days until the Senate vote, with a minimum of 14 days and a maximum of 153 days, with a standard deviation of 34 days. Splitting the data in search of trends indicates ideology is an interesting criterion. As indicated in Figure 2.1, conservatives, on average, wait approximately 65 days until confirmation. Meanwhile, liberals wait only 47 days until confirmation. As such, it seems clear to investigate these phenomena further to confirm whether there is an ideological divide when it comes to the confirmation process.

Table 2.1 Regression Results for Effects of Ideology on Judicial Nominations

Independent Variables	*Coefficient*
Ideology	−3.44 (18.29)
Qualifications	−71.34 (24.2)
Chief Justice	11.56 (17.79)
Party	12.08 (18.08)
President	28.95 (14.32)
Recess	−1.8 (1.35)
Constant	158.66 (49.86)

N = 30
$R^2 = .75$
Chi square = 363.55
Df = 75
Source: Model Constructed by DePlato, Justin using Data from the Supreme Court Compendium.

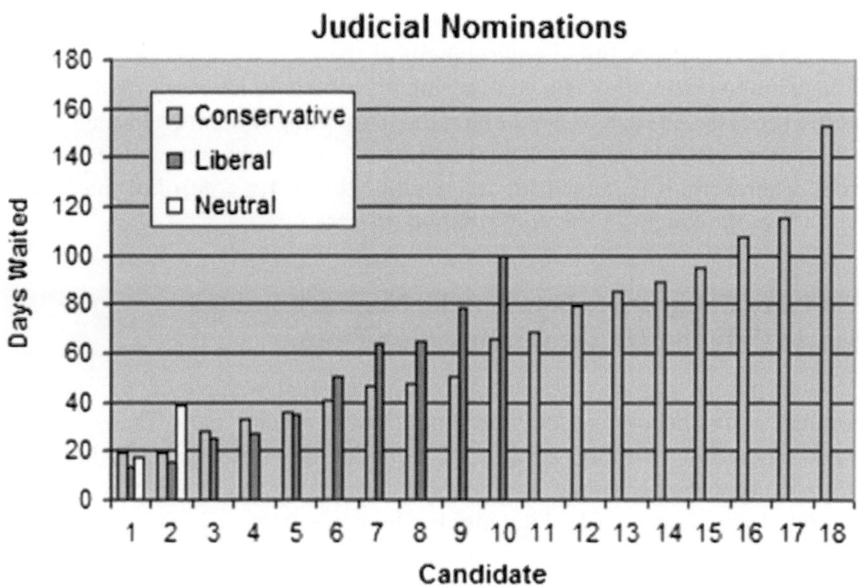

Figure 2.1 *Source:* Author compiled using the Supreme Court Compendium.

THE ARGUMENT

Americans often want to think that the United States Senate is not as overtly a political institution as the House of Representatives, and we think this is especially true when discussing the judicial nomination process. Perhaps this is due to the nature of the individuals being nominated—Supreme Court Justices. We may conclude that, since it is the appointment and confirmation of a member of the apolitical branch of government, the process should be apolitical. However, this conclusion couldn't be further from the truth. One does not have to go back very far in history to see evidence of the insidious and vitriolic political process currently consuming the Senate confirmation process of Supreme Court Justices. Mr. Bork in 1986 was shot down over political cleavages between himself and liberal democrat Senators. Clarence Thomas barely survived the onslaught from the left during his confirmation process. Harriet Miers withdrew her name amidst the continued partisan assault from ideologically opposed senators. Such examples make it fairly clear that partisanship and ideology have some effect on the process; but to what extent?

TESTABLE HYPOTHESES

As has been already mentioned, scholars have long suggested partisanship has an effect on the judicial confirmation process (Friedman 1983; Segal 1987). Further, the political environment of the Senate would be an obvious dimension to start with when considering the effects of ideology on the nomination process. As such, it would be rather surprising if democrat senators did not support democratic presidential nominees, and vice versa with conservatives. Therefore, it is reasonable to conclude that party control of the Senate will affect the length of the confirmation process.

H1: Party Congruence Between the Nominee and the Senate Will Shorten the Confirmation Process

Despite purely partisan concerns, the intellectual values of the judicial nominees have become much more important in recent years. The American Bar Association candidly scores each nominee determining his or her relative ideology. For example, the confirmation process of Justice Sotomayor exhibited the nature of ideology and the Senate's interest in determining the judge's ideology prior to confirmation. As such, it is reasonable to construe ideological composition of the Senate will affect the length of the confirmation process.

H2: Ideology Congruence Between the Nominee and the Senate Will Shorten the Confirmation Process

Anti-presidential motivations may also be a factor explaining the length of the confirmation process. Scholars have suggested these motivations are more likely to surface when the president is weak (Halper 1972; Schmidhauser and Berg 1972). A president is weakest during the final year of his term, notably the fourth year. Therefore, it is reasonable to construe the timing of a nomination in relation to the president's term will affect the length of the confirmation process.

H3: The Confirmation Process Will Be Longer During a President's Fourth Year

Scholars have long suggested presidential coattails aide congruent party members during a presidential election (Scigliano 1971). Scholars have also examined whether such coattails would aid a president in succeeding with judicial confirmations (Frank 1941; Murphy 1962; and Scigliano 1971). The implication is that as a president's electoral margin increases so does the likelihood of a successful confirmation. Therefore, it is reasonable to construe that a president's electoral victory may have an effect on the length of a confirmation process.

DATA AND METHODS

The data gathered for this study was gathered from the *United States Supreme Court Compendium*. The data gathered indicates incidences of judicial confirmations/nominees since 1950. For all the observations made of the judicial confirmation process the following information was gathered:

1. Number of days from nomination to Senate vote
2. Segal and Cover score[3] for Judicial Ideology of Nominee
3. Partisan Composition of the Senate
4. President's party affiliation
5. President's electoral votes
6. Age of Nominee
7. Gender of Nominee
8. Race of Nominee
9. ABA judicial score

The dependent variable in this study is the number of days from the nomination of a judicial candidate until the Senate vote. Regardless of confirmation or rejection, the measure in this study is to account for the amount of time it takes for a judicial nominee to receive an up or down vote on their candidacy. In so doing, this study allows us to infer that the length of the process can speak to the degree of contention for a candidate. Whereby in measuring the length of the process by association of ideology it can be inferred if ideology causes a lengthening of the process.

In order to test the hypotheses mentioned in this chapter we constructed an OLS regression to determine the parameter estimates and their effects on the dependent variable. An OLS regression is a method to model numerical data obtained from observations by adjusting the parameters of the model, thus producing the "best" fit line or optimal fit of the data as related to the observations. The best fit is characterized by the sum of the squared residuals having the least value. The underlying assumption of the model is that experimental errors have a normal distribution. In simplest terms the OLS model aims to find a value a^ and a b^ of the parameters "a" (intercept) and "b" (slope).

The following model was constructed:

Y = b1 + b2I + b3L + b4V + b5A + b6M + e
Y = Number of days from nomination of nominee to Senate vote
I = Ideology of judicial nominee (coded using Segal and Cover Scores)
P = Partisan composition of Senate (coded 1 if a majority of the Senate is controlled by the president's party, 0 if otherwise)
E = Presidential Electoral Vote
G = Judicial nominee demographics (1 if minority, 0 if otherwise)
C = Judicial Credentials (ABA score for each nominee)

FURTHER NOTE ON METHODOLOGY

To control for any autocorrelation, we use robust standard errors. While we may be concerned that an OLS regression analysis, analyzing variables across time, could cause heteroscasticidity, in this model, since the robust SE are used, along with acknowledging that the number of observations is limited, therefore making the method appropriate and the only limited form available.

Due to the limited observations, the OLS model is an expanded ANOVA model whereby we are able to capture the variance of the variables, over time, in a limited capacity. Therefore, we are unable to foster generalizable conclusions from the data, but can at least capture the change and variance of the variables, over time. We may not construe correlations, though; the patterned behavior is convincing to be used as a determinate for future nomination predictions.

FINDINGS AND DISCUSSION

Below, in Figure 2.1, are the results from the OLS regression and its estimates. The results show that there is an inherent liberal bias, which means that, more likely than not, liberal bias will exist on the Bench, causing harm to conservative jurisprudence principles. The model was built to capture the effect of the compositional variables on the Senate's nomination process for Supreme Court Justices and Chief Justices (CJ). The results below, as an analysis of variance, indicate only patterns of behavior and, because of the lack of observations, our results do not report statistical significance.

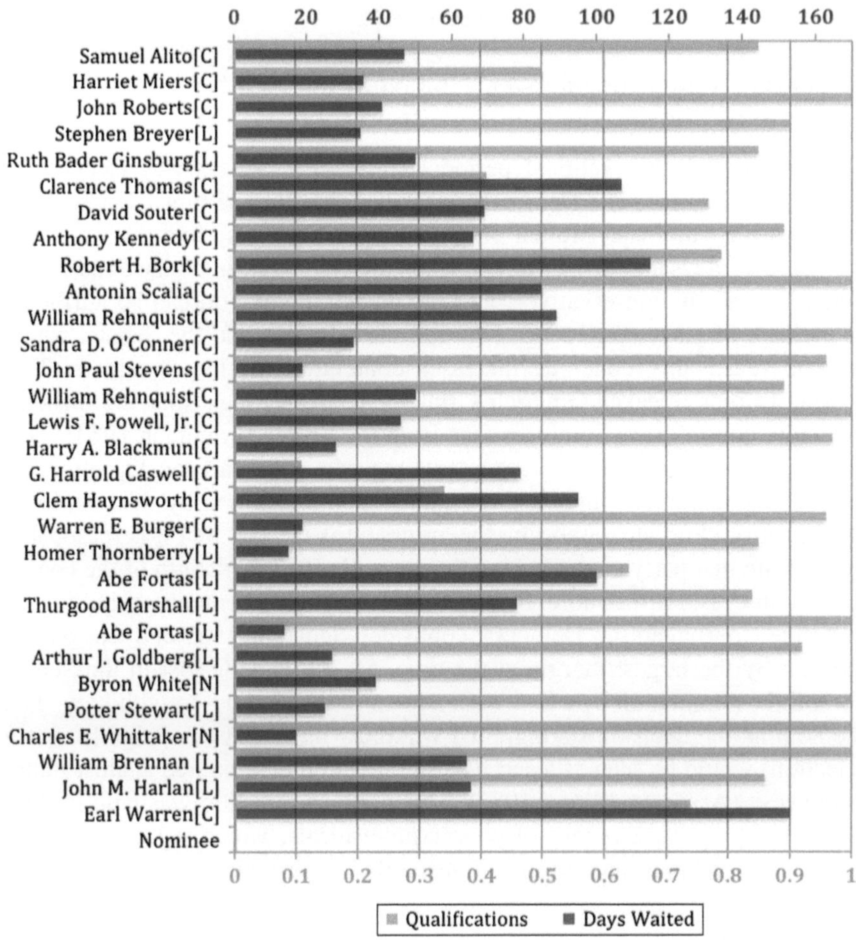

Figure 2.2 *Source:* Author compiled using the Supreme Court Compendium.

On the value of qualifications (Figure 2.2), ranging from 0 to 1, 0 being least qualified and 1 being most qualified, our data shows for every .1 reduction in the qualification score (meaning moving from 1 to 0), the nomination would increase by 71 days. Hence, perfect scores of 1 (most qualified), would have a 71 percent shorter nomination process. Based on the raw data this would equate to about a 100-day shorter nomination process. On the measure of CJ, the regression indicates that a Chief Justices's nomination process would be 11 days longer than an associate justice. This illustrates a conservative justice—who has below average qualifications—will have a much harder time getting confirmed, whereas a liberal judge will find it easier, on average, to be confirmed. This implies that there is an inherent liberal bias at play, which means that, more likely than not, liberal bias will exist on the Bench.

IDEOLOGY

H1: Party Congruence Between the Nominee and the Senate Will Shorten the Confirmation Process

Throughout the observational period covered, the Senate was Republican controlled nine times and Democrat controlled the other 22 times. On average, conservative candidates waited 16 days longer for a vote and the wait time increased 17 days above the average when the GOP controlled the Senate. The noted increase in conservative wait time during this period can be attributed to the lack of party congruence between the nominee and the Senate, which we can reasonably conclude increases contention for the candidate. This affirms former Speaker Gingrich's statement (2009) regarding the difficulties more conservative nominees face from the Senate (Friedman 1983). This also validates Segal's (1987) arguments regarding the partisanship effect on judicial nominations, which are strengthened and affirmed by this empirical investigation. Further supporting the argument is the fact that it is reasonable to construe that party control of the Senate will affect the length of the confirmation process. Furthermore, Robert Bork led a highly contentious bid for the Supreme Court against a Democrat controlled Senate in 1987 and was denied the seat by the largest margin at the time, 58–42. Having lost in the Senate committee nomination by a 9–5 vote, Bork still decided not to withdraw from the nomination decision stating, "If I withdraw now, that campaign [partisan rejection] would be seen as a success, and it would be mounted against future nominees" (Associated Press 1987). This partisan rejection was held in light of Bork's long track record of conservative ideals, which went against the Senate's liberal bias, and ultimately made the confirmation attempt a failure.

H2: Ideology Congruence Between the Nominee and the Senate Will Shorten the Confirmation Process

The interpretation on the OLS regression shows ideology ranging from 0 to 1, 0–.49 being conservative, .51–1 being liberal, and .5 being neutral, in association with days waited for nomination confirmation or denial. For every .10 reduction in ideology (meaning moving from 1 to 0, liberal to conservative), the length of days increased by 3. Therefore, a conservative nominee will have, roughly, a 30 percent longer confirmation period than a liberal nominee. Based on the raw data, the range was from 153 to 14, interpreted meaning a conservative would have, roughly, a 45-day longer confirmation process (153*.30). In support, Sandra Day O'Connor and John Roberts, each conservative and highly qualified (each with a 1 on the qualification scale), had shorter than average appointment times, 33 and 41 days respectively. Empirical investigation suggests this feat is owed to the ideological congruence between conservative candidates and a republican controlled Senate. When the senate was Democrat controlled, the greatest number of days waited is attributed to Earl Warren, who was a conservative going against the opposite party's ideology. Harriet Miers also led a failed attempt at landing a seat on the Supreme Court's bench because the Republican held Senate challenged the depth of her conservative values. Miers nomination came at a time when many republicans saw the need for a strong conservative nomination to the Supreme Court to reestablish President Bush's control over the selection process. This lack of congruence between Miers' ideology with Senate Republicans emphasizes our findings.

H3: The Confirmation Process Will Be Longer During a President's Final Year of a Given Term

The data show that when the president is in their last year of a term, the process is about 28 days longer, which reinforces the notion that presidential electoral victories influence the length of the confirmation process. Highlighting these phenomena, Earl Warren and Robert Bork were both nominated in a president's last year and their wait times were well above the average, 153 and 115 days respectively, revealing that the confirmation process is longer during a president's final year in a term. Abe Fortas' nomination to Chief Justice by President Lyndon Johnson in 1968 highlights the lame-duck effect on presidential appointment and subsequent Senate confirmation of candidates. Five months before the next presidential election, Chief Justice Earl Warren informed the president he was retiring and Abe Fortas was nominated to be his replacement. Republicans and conservative democrats essentially used the threat of a filibuster to block Fortas's nomination to Supreme Court Justice because of his close ties to Johnson, liberal bias, and in hopes Nixon would win and appoint someone else. Similar tactics were observed recently with Merrick Garland.

CONCLUSION

In this chapter we argued that the United States Senate played a pivotal role in the politicization of the Supreme Court. In support of this argument, we adduced that there was an obvious liberal bias in Justice and Chief Justice nominations from the Senate, and that a liberal judge will find it easier, on average, to be confirmed than a conservative, despite their respective qualifications. Conservative justices have a much harder time getting confirmed, and this effect is compounded if they are less qualified or have ideals that differ from that of the Senate majority's. This means that, more often than not, there will be a liberal bias on the bench, which seems to increase the likelihood that left-wing principles of jurisprudence are adopted on the Bench. This liberal bias on the Bench can further be attributed to the general nature of the Senate to be Democrat controlled and the inherent correlation between shorter confirmation times and an ideological alignment between the nominee and Senate majority. The support for each hypothesis via our OLS regression model reveals the politicized nature of the appointment and confirmation process of Supreme Court Justices. Our findings cast light on the nature of the partisan assaults taking place throughout this process and reveal the lack of objectivity regarding Supreme Court Justice selection. In light of this political revelation, our findings further support the need for future conservative nominees to be well qualified to have a better chance of surviving the partisan onslaught.

As things stand at the time of publication, two significant events relevant to our major thesis have occurred. Judge Merrick Garland, the nominee of President Obama, was prevented from becoming the replacement of the late Justice Scalia by means of a successful tactic by Senate Republicans; the Senate Republicans avoided voting to approve *or* reject Judge Garland—taking political advantage of their Constitutional duty to give advice and consent—effectively stalling the nomination process such that President Trump was able to select a nominee instead. There was much fanfare during the employment of this tactic. Soon after the Republicans began to stall the process, a 1992 video of Vice President Joe Biden, then a senator, surfaced; this video depicted the senator arguing in favor of delaying the confirmation of one of President Bush Sr.'s nominees until the presidential election was over;[4] similar arguments have since been made by Senate Republicans. The situation was in many ways highly ironical.

Senate Republicans under President Donald Trump have not faced the same problems. Although the Senate Democrats attempted a filibuster of the nomination of Judge Neil Gorsuch, they lacked the numbers for this strategy to succeed. Senate majority leader Mitch McConnell invoked what is colloquially known as the "nuclear option"—a motion, approved by a simple majority (50% + 1 votes), to reduce the threshold of votes required to successfully nominate a new Supreme Court Justice to the Supreme Court to be itself a simple majority, rather than a supermajority (at least 60 of 100 votes)—and as a result Gorsuch was nominated by a simple majority of Senate Republicans. This option was not available to Senate Democrats at the time that President Obama had nominated Judge Garland to the Court, since the Democrats at that time were a minority in the Senate—the nuclear option would have only helped the republicans. In another bout of irony, the nuclear option had at one point helped Senate Democrats secure the appointment of several federal appellate court judges that President Obama had nominated.

The process had thus been reversed on Senate Democrats by Senate Republicans to President Trump's advantage. Neil Gorsuch, despite the attempted filibuster, was nominated and confirmed by Senate Republicans to the Supreme Court of the United States, becoming the 113th Justice of the Court.

The process of Gorsuch's nomination was fraught with politicization—as has been nearly every aspect of President Trump's presidency and the attendant press frenzy. It is not uncommon for political opponents to dredge up the best possible evidence against nominees that they disagree with, but the politicization in Gorsuch's case was astonishing. For example, a cursory internet search for "Trump fascism" returns too many relevant results to count. As such, it was not entirely surprising when, during the nomination process, Judge Gorsuch was painted with the fascist brush. A specious and spurious claim made in the *Daily Mail* by Alana Goodman claimed that Gorsuch had founded a club for the promotion of far-right political stances called "Fascism Forever."[5] The news report, however, was categorically false, since the club was a mere joke on the part of Gorsuch.[6] Opposition research against Supreme Court nominees is par for the course—but fabrications on the basis of political narratives formed around the sitting President seem to mark even more clearly the extent to which the nomination process has been politicized in recent years.

The legitimacy of these tactics is disputed on constitutional and traditionalistic bases; whether it is legitimate is not a question we address here, but it is certainly to be taken as yet another piece of evidence that the process of nomination and confirmation is highly politicized. We remark more explicitly on the politicization of advice and consent in the conclusion of this book.

NOTES

1. A custom of the United States Senate of refusing to confirm a presidential appointment of an official in or from a state when the appointment is opposed by the senators or senior senator of the president's party from that state (*Merriam-Webster* n.d.).
2. A lame duck refers to a politician who is approaching the end of his or her term and a successor has already been chosen. A lame duck can occur when a politician has lost reelection, decided to retire, abandoned office, or has exhausted his or her term limit (Benz n.d.).
3. See Segal and Cover (1989) for the original scores; see Segal, et al. for an elaboration on the original data (1995).
4. See Biden (1992).
5. See Goodman (2017).
6. See LaCapria (2017).

BIBLIOGRAPHY

Abraham, Henry. *Justices & Presidents: A Political History of Appointments to the Supreme Court*. New York: Oxford University Press, 1974.

Associated Press. "Bork Gives Reasons for Continuing Fight." *The New York Times*, October 10, 1987.

Baum, Lawrence. *The Supreme Court*. Washington, DC: Congressional Quarterly Press, 1981.

Benz, Rainer. "Lame Duck in Politics: Definition and Overview." study.com. n.d.

Biden, Joe. 1992. https://www.realclearpolitics.com/video/2016/02/22/biden_in_1992_bush_should_not_name_a_nominee_until_after_the_november_election.html.

Cole, Kenneth. "The Role of the Senate in Confirmation of Judicial Nominations." *American Political Science Review* 28 (1934): 875–94.

Danelski, David. *A Supreme Court Justice Is Appointed*. New York: Random House, 1964.

Edwards, George. *Presidential Influence in Congress*. San Francisco: W. H. Freeman, 1980.

Epstein, Lee, and Jeffrey A. Segal. *Advice and Consent: The Politics of Judicial Appointments*. Oxford: Oxford University Press, 2007.

Farrar, Donald E., and Robert R. Glauber. "Multicollinearity in Regression Analysis: The Problem Revisited." *Review of Economics and Statistics* 49, 1 (February 1967): 92–107.

Frank, John P. "The Appointment of Supreme Court Justices: Prestige, Principles and Politics." *Wisconsin Law Review* (1941): 172–210.

Friedman, Richard D. "The Transformation in Senate Response to Supreme Court Nominations: From Reconstruction to the Taft Administration and Beyond." *Cardozo Law Review* 5 (1983): 1–95.

Gingrich, Newt. Interview by Greta Van Susteren. *The World According to Newt Gingrich*. FOX News Network, LLC. Fox News. May 1, 2009.

Goodman, Alana. "EXCLUSIVE: Trump's Supreme Court Pick Founded and Led Club Called 'Fascism Forever' at His Elite All-Boys." Washington Prep School. February 2, 2017. http://archive.is/8Z99g (accessed February 4, 2018).

Grossman, Joel B., and Stephen L. Wasby. "The Senate and Supreme Court Nominations: Some Reflections." *Duke Law Journal* 21, 3 (1972): 557–91.

Halper, Thomas. "Senate Rejection of Supreme Court Nominees." *Drake Law Review* 22 (1972): 102–13.

Haynes, George. *The Senate of the United States*. Vol. II. II Vols. New York: Russell and Russell, 1960.

LaCapria, Kim. "Snopes: Did Neil Gorsuch Found a High School 'Fascism Forever' Club?" February 3, 2017. https://www.snopes.com/neil-gorsuchs-fascism-forever-club/ (accessed February 4, 2018).

McHargue, Daniel S. *Factors Influencing the Selection and Appointment of Members of the United States Supreme Court, 1789–1932*. Los Angeles: University of California Press, 1949.

Merriam-Webster. "Senatorial Courtesy." *The Merriam-Webster Dictionary*. Merriam-Webster Incorporated, n.d.

Murphey, Walter F. *Congress and the Court: A Case Study in the American Political Process*. Chicago: University of Chicago Press, 1962.

Pritchett, C. Herman. *Congress versus the Supreme Court, 1957–1960*. Minneapolis: University of Minnesota Press, 1961.

Schmidhauser, John R. *Judges and Justices: The Federal Appellate Judiciary*. Boston: Little, Brown, and Company, 1979.

Schmidhauser, John R., and Larry L. Berg. *The Supreme Court and Congress*. New York: Free Press, 1972.

Scigliano, Robert G. *The Supreme Court and the Presidency*. New York: Free Press, 1971.

Segal, Jeffrey. "Senate Confirmation of Supreme Court Justices: Partisan and Institutional Politics." *The Journal of Politics* 49, 4 (November 1987): 998–1015.

Segal, Jeffrey A., and Albert D. Cover. "Ideological Values and the Votes of U.S. Supreme Court Justices." *The American Political Science Review* 83, 2 (June 1989): 557–65.

Segal, Jeffrey A., Lee Epstein, Charles M. Cameron, and Harold J. Spaeth. "Ideological Values and the Votes of U.S. Supreme Court Justices Revisited." *The Journal of Politics* 57, 3 (August 1995): 812–23.

Spaeth, Harold J. *Supreme Court Policy Making: Explanation and Prediction*. San Francisco: W. H. Freeman & Co. Ltd., 1979.

Tanenhaus, Joseph, and Walter F. Murphey. "Patterns of Public Support for the Supreme Court: a Panel Study." *The Journal of Politics* 43, 1 (February 1981): 24–39.

Warren, Charles. *The Supreme Court in United States History*. III vols. Boston: Little, Brown, and Company, 1922.

Chapter 3

The Diminishing Docket

Since the late 1980s, there has been a major decline in the number of cases that the U.S. Supreme Court decides each term (see Figure 3.1). The diminishing Supreme Court docket has received extensive media and scholarly attention and yet, despite this increased awareness, scholars have not been able to convincingly explain why the docket has diminished so substantially. Even though Chemerinsky (2007) contends that there is "no obvious explanation" for the decrease, there have been a number of hypotheses advanced by scholars, the media, and even the justices themselves to explain the shrinking docket. Some of the explanations relate to factors external to the Court, while others suggest that internal dynamics or institutional factors are the cause of this decline.

Addressing the puzzle of why the Court is hearing fewer and fewer cases is of great importance. Several scholars argue that the diminishing docket will have major ramifications on the legal community and the country as a whole. Starr (2006) argues that this trend has had negative effects on federal law by making it less and less clear since the law is being interpreted less and less by the high Court. He also argues that, because of this, the Court has neglected its duty to bring uniformity to the law. Similarly, Chemerinsky (2007) contends that if the Court does not resolve legal conflicts among the U.S. Courts of Appeals, then interpretive disagreements will continue to fester in the lower courts.

The drop in the number of cases has been quite dramatic. The Court issued 151 signed opinions in 1982, while in 2006 the number of cases dwindled to 67. The Hughes and Stone Courts issued an average of about 152 and 142 signed opinions each term, while the Rehnquist Court issued only about 95 per term (see Figure 3.2).

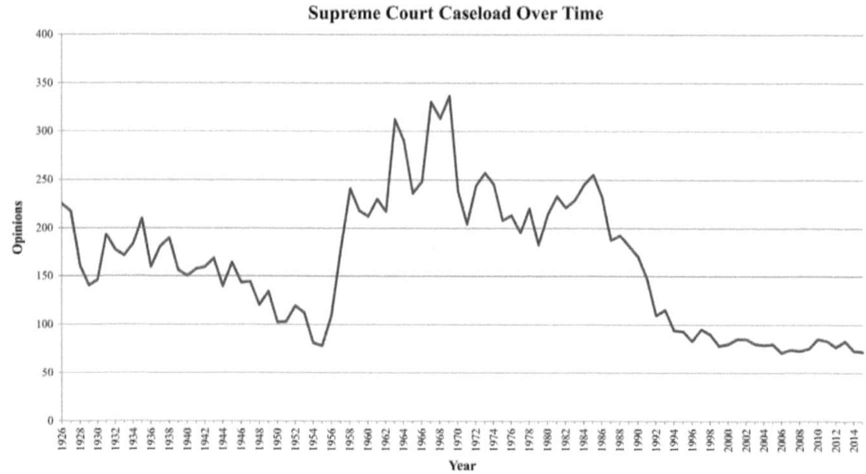

Figure 3.1 *Source:* Author compiled using the Supreme Court Compendium.

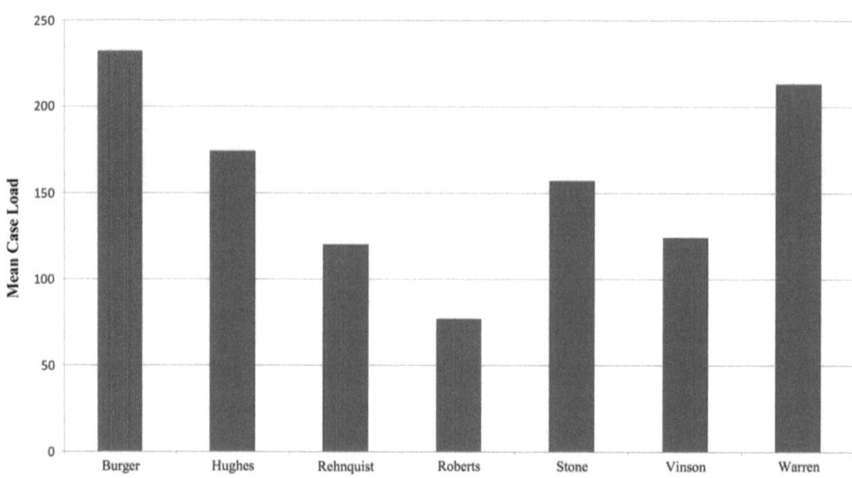

Figure 3.2 *Source:* Author compiled using the Supreme Court Compendium.

This drop in caseload has not been accompanied by an increase in workload. Parker (1999) examined the length of time it takes to decide cases and the length in pages of decisions during the Rehnquist Court and finds that workload does not appear to have increased. As some commentators have already suggested, the decrease in docket size may actually indicate a reduction in the amount work that is being accomplished.

This change has attracted attention from journalists (Greenhouse 2006; Lane 2004) and even the justices themselves. In a speech before the Third

Circuit's judicial conference, justice David Souter noted the diminishing docket and said that there was no "conscious decision" to reduce the number of cases they hear (Duffy 1995). He suggested that this decrease may be due to factors external to the Court, such as ideological homogeneity among the federal courts which had led to fewer inter-circuit disagreements.

Despite the large amount of attention paid to the diminishing docket, it has been subject to little rigorous empirical study. The majority of the work on the diminishing case load has been done by scholars in the legal profession, not political scientists (Chemerinsky 2007; Cordray and Cordray 2001; Hellman 1996; Starr 2006). Scott (2006) has been the only scholar to study this question with statistical modeling and, although he did not find support for most of the hypotheses, he did find evidence that the composition of the Court matters a great deal. Specifically, he found that Justices Byron White and Harry Blackmun motioned to hear more cases than the other justices with which they served. Their retirement was associated with a major decrease in docket size.

Scholars have frequently argued that the change in docket size is due mainly to the retirement and replacement of the justices sitting on the Court. Cordray and Cordray (2001) call it one of the most "compelling" explanations of the change in docket size. They contend that the retirement of six justices between 1986 and 1994 was the major cause of the reduction in docket size. Scott (2006) argues that it was the voting patterns of Justice White and Justice Blackmun in particular who influenced the growth in docket size during the Burger Court. According to the argument, White felt strongly that the Supreme Court should supervise the federal courts and resolve inter-circuit conflicts and therefore would vote to grant more cases. The reasons for Blackmun wanting to hear more cases are less clear, but O'Brien (1997a) found that Blackmun had one of the highest rates of Joining-3 votes, implying that he would be willing to grant review if other justices would. However, Scott studied only signed opinions that examined issues which came from the federal courts. He looked only at these cases because he was testing the interaction between the Supreme Court and the federal courts.

In contrast, there are other justices who operate very differently from Justices Blackmun and White. Justice John Paul Stevens has been one of the most vocal opponents of the Court hearing too many cases. In fact, he once suggested that the "rule of four" ought to become the "rule of five" in order to help reduce the number of cases the Court hears (Stevens 1983). It would be difficult to determine, but Stevens may have impressed upon his younger colleagues that a large docket is not desirable.

There is a large empirical literature on what factors influence the Supreme Court to hear certain types of cases, but few have addressed the macroscopic issues associated with the size of the docket. Scholars know a great deal about the factors that influence which cases the Court hears, but very little on what determines the size of the docket. Furthermore, scholars have explored the role of the solicitor general (Bailey, Kamoie and Maltzman 2005).

In addition, there has been empirical verification that whether or not an *amicus curiae* brief is filed along with a case influences its inclusion on the Supreme Court's plenary docket (Caldeira and Wright 1988, 1990; McGuire 1994; Segal and Reedy 1988). Finally, the Supreme Court responds to particular cues that are often associated with salient cases (Songer 1979; Songer, Cameron, and Segal 1995).

THE ARGUMENT

Even though scholars have been paying increased attention to the diminishing docket, many questions remain unanswered. There are several hypotheses that have been repeatedly discussed in the literature, but there is little consensus concerning which one has the greatest explanatory value.

The hypothesis that has received the most attention deals with the composition of the Court. This hypothesis posits that as new justices replace old justices, voting patterns will change and thus influence the number of cases the Court agrees to review. O'Brien (1997a, 1997b, 2005) has been one of the most forceful advocates of this hypothesis. He has emphasized the importance of composition of the Court and the effect it has on the Court's decision to hear cases. For example, O'Brien (2005, 137) stressed the importance of each new justice of the Rehnquist court having been appointed from the U.S. Court of Appeals and therefore likely to "defer issues" to those courts and not involve itself in inter-circuit disputes. Although he does not extend this argument, the experience of serving on a federal circuit court apparently makes a justice less likely to grant review in certain cases.

H1: As the Supreme Court's Mean Ideology Becomes More Conservative the Docket Size Will Decrease

Related to the composition of the Court are adjustments in the mean ideological values of the justices. These changes may have an effect on the docket size (Hellman 1996). The ideology of the Supreme Court is important for explaining judicial behavior. Collective behavior determines docket size through the rule of four, which is the tradition that four justices must agree to hear a case before it is put on the docket. Therefore investigating the effect of ideology on the docket size is essential. Ideology is determined by utilizing the scores created by Segal and Cover (1989).

The rationale for ideology being a factor in docket size rests on the distinction between judicial activism and restraint. Scholars have argued that conservative justices tend to be more likely to show judicial restraint, the more liberal a justice is the more likely they are to act actively on the bench. As an extension, ideology as an explanatory factor in this research draws from the structural factor that justices determine their docket. Therefore, considering judicial ideological tendencies toward "agenda setting" or plenary docket size is an important endeavor.

H2: The Elimination of Mandatory Jurisdiction is Associated with a Reduction in the Supreme Court's Docket Size

The diminished docket may also be due to changes in the Supreme Court's mandatory jurisdiction. The Judicial Improvements and Access to Justice Act of 1988 eliminated most of the Court's mandatory appellate jurisdiction. Scholars have debated the impact that this act made on the docket size. Some argue that it had little effect (Cordray and Cordray 2001; Hellman 1996). Yet, intuitively, it would make sense that it would have an effect on docket size since it changed a part of the institutional nature of the case selection process.

H3: An Increase in the Number of Presidential Vetoes Will Lead to a Drop in the Number of Cases Heard by the Supreme Court

An interesting hypothesis that has yet to be explored was suggested in a speech by Justice David Souter. He suggested that the number of cases that the Court hears may have decreased because Reagan and Bush vetoed a number of statutes, which reduced the supply of these important cases (Duffy 1995, 28). The logic behind this argument is that if the president removes a portion of the controversial legislation passed by Congress, there is a reduction in the pool of statutes that would likely be appealed to the Supreme Court. We would expect this to manifest itself after several years since litigation takes time to manifest; there is no way a case challenging congressional legislation would make it to the Supreme Court the same year it was passed. For instance, the Brady Handgun Violence Protection Act was passed in 1993, and the case that challenged it, *Prince v. United States*, was not decided until 1997, four years later. Similarly, the Violence Against Women Act was passed in 1994 and *United States v. Morrison* was not decided until 2000, 6 years later. Again, these examples show how long it takes before non-vetoed legislation makes it to the Court. Scholars have not systematically examined the effect of presidential vetoes on the Supreme Court's docket.

H4: At Points of Ideological Incongruence Between Two Courts, We Expect an Increase in Docket Size to Ensue

We argue that, as the Supreme Court's composition changes ideologically, from a previous Court to an ensuing Court, that the justices may be more likely to overturn past precedent. Therefore, at points of ideological incongruence between two distinctly opposing ideological Courts—for example, the Warren Court versus the Burger Court—the likelihood of the ensuing Court to pursue a "new" agenda or direction for the Court should manifest itself as an increase in docket size. This argument is drawn from literature regarding institutional theories on the presidency and the underlying effect ideological congruence, or lack thereof, has on the president's ability to govern. Theoretically, if we consider the Court as an institution, we can extend and test whether similar institutional factors of congruency, or lack thereof in terms of the presidency, will have a similar effect on the Court as the Court's composition changes, and, as such, affect its agenda setting patterns (Moe 1985).

H5: The Older the Mean Age of the Court, the Fewer Cases They Will Hear

Another reason for changes in the docket size may be due to the average age of Supreme Court justices. Scott (2006) included a variable that captured the average of the Court. The argument behind this variable is that as justices age they become less productive as they age and become reluctant to hear a large number of cases.

DATA AND METHODOLOGY

Our data for the model was gathered from the Supreme Court Compendium. The data compiled only indicates incidences of docket size since 1953. For all of the observations made concerning the U.S. Supreme Court's docket size, the following information was gathered:

1. Number of signed opinions per term (caseload)
2. Segal and Spaeth Ideology score per justice
3. The Judicial Improvements and Access to Justice Act of 1988
4. Number of Presidential Vetoes per Court Term
5. Age of Justice per year
6. Court's Mean Ideology Score

The dependent variable in this study is the number of signed opinions of the Court. Therefore, we do not include decisions that were remanded without argument and per curium opinions. In order to test the hypotheses mentioned in this chapter we constructed an OLS regression to determine the parameter estimates and their effects on the dependent variable. The following model was constructed:

$$Y = b1 + b2I + b3L + b4V + b5A + b6M + e$$

Where:

Y = Supreme Court Docket (Total number of signed opinions per Court, per term)
I = Segal and Cover Scores
L = 1.The Judicial Improvements and Access to Justice Act of 1988 (coded 1 for years following 1988, 0 if before 1988)
V = Number of Vetoes per presidency during a Court term, lagged 4 years
A = Average Age of the Court per term
M= Ideological Congruence or Congruence between Courts (coded 0 at points of congruence, coded 1 at points of incongruence). (Incongruence or congruence is defined using the mean ideological values of the Court in comparison to the previous Court.)

The first independent variable is mean Supreme Court ideology. This variable was operationalized using Segal and Cover scores. The second variable controls for the Judicial Improvements and Access to Justice Act of 1988. This act rid the Court of most of its mandatory jurisdiction. It is operationalized using a dummy variable for the years after the act was passed. The third independent variable deals with the effect of presidential vetoes. One would not expect the effect to manifest itself for several years. Therefore we created a four-year lead variable using the number of vetoes per year. The fourth variable is the average age of the Court. The variable was constructed by taking the age of each justice each term and calculating the mean. The fifth variable deals with congruency between courts. The variable was constructed by assessing the mean ideological of the Court, versus the previous Court. Periods in which the mean ideological value of the Court changed dramatically from either positive to negative, or vice versa, were coded 1 = point of ideological incongruence 0 = point of ideological congruence.

To control for the potential problem of correlated observations (residuals), we used robust standard errors while clustering the standard errors. This was done because the risk for heteroscedasticity was higher than usual because our data set had observations across time, all of which may lead to our parameter estimates being "optimistic."

FINDINGS AND DISCUSSION

Below, in Table 3.1, are the results from the OLS regression and its estimates. We suggested in this chapter that institutional factors in the Supreme Court

Table 3.1 OLS Regression Results of Multi Variable Effects on Court Docket

Independent Variables	*Coefficient*
Court ideology	–37.528**
	(11.940)
Judicial Act of 1988	–48.781***
	(11.040)
Presidential Veto	–.373*
	(.1949)
Age	.227
	(.5143)
Incongruence	12.975*
	(7.540)
Constant	107.206***
	(26.753)
$R^2 = .668$	
N = 56	

Dependent Variable: Number of signed opinions per Court, per Term.
P < .01***; p < .05**; p < .10*, two-tailed test.

create a possibility in which the composition of the Court might be a leading determinate in understanding the Court's docket size, per term. As such our model was built to capture the effect of compositional variables on the total number of signed opinions the Court signed, per term.

As reported above in Table 3.1, our model yielded some interesting results. In order to simplify the discussion we have broken down the findings below per hypothesis.

H1: As the Supreme Court's Mean Ideology Becomes More Conservative the Docket Size Will Decrease

Our most significant finding and in line with our principle thesis is that ideology has an effect on the Supreme Court's docket size. We suggest that a conservative Court, as defined by the mean Segal and Cover score for the Court, will hear fewer cases than a liberal Court. We suggested this because conservative actors often yield an approach less interested in offering "good public policy" and as such less interested in "legislating" from the bench. Our theory is in accordance with literature explaining congressional behavior as a result of ideological differences which yields different levels of legislative activity (Campbell 1982; Fenno 1973); it also accords with theories explaining judicial preference for public policy positions expressed either through an activist or restraining Court (Mishler and Sheehan 1993).

As evidenced in Table 3.1, a conservative Court will hear fewer cases than a liberal Court. Our finding of a –37 beta score indicates that as the mean ideology of the Court moves .10 units towards the conservative end of the spectrum such a Court will hear 37 fewer cases then if the inverse occurred. This finding confirms our theoretical argument that the diminishing Court docket size is highly correlated with the ideological compositional change in the Court over the last 50 years.

H2: The Elimination of Mandatory Jurisdiction is Associated with a Reduction in the Supreme Court's Docket Size

Earlier in this chapter, we argued that the Judicial Improvements and Access to Justice Act of 1988 would have a negative effect on the Court's docket size following the implementation of the legal measure. The primary task of the Act was to decrease the number of petitions to the Court by making the certiorari process more defined, thus making petitions easily rendered as having no "legal standing." Our findings in Table 3.1, in fact, indicate that the Act did have the expected effect on the Court's docket size as it has aided in the diminishing docket. As reported in Table 3.1, Courts following the Act have heard 48 fewer cases than the Courts which preceded the Act.

H3: An Increase in the Number of Presidential Vetoes Will Lead to a Drop in the Number of Cases Heard by the Supreme Court

As we suggested, the number of cases the Court hears, and consequently the resulting signed opinions, are affected by the number of presidential vetoes. While leading the variable 4 years (allowing for the veto to manifest its effect on docket size), our finding confirms a remark offered by Justice Souter who suggested that the number of cases the Court deliberates on may have decreased because Reagan and Bush vetoed a number of statutes (Duffy 1995, 28). The finding in Table 3.1 indicates that for every 10 presidential vetoes the docket size declined by approximately 3 signed opinions (beta –.373).

H4: At Points of Ideological Incongruence Between Two Courts We Expect an Increase in Docket Size to Ensue

We suggested that periods of ideological incongruence between Courts might lead to spikes in docket size simply because the incoming Court is interested in overturning previous precedent set forth by the previous Court. As indicated in Table 3.1, our finding is correct to account for the effects of this unique period on the Court. The finding indicates that at points of ideological incongruence the incoming Court will be likely to hear more cases than the previous Court (Perry 1991).

Since, in our data set, there is only one available period in which this effect took place, we are specifically explaining the spike in cases heard by the Burger Court in the 1970s. Our findings relate well to the message of President Nixon that new Chief Justice Burger would seek to reduce the "pro-criminal" agenda of the Warren Court; one might then surmise that it would be expected that the Burger Court would pursue cases that would overturn previous precedent.

H5: As the Mean Age of the Court Increases, the Fewer Cases the Court Will Hear

The remaining explanatory variable, age, was not statistically significant. This is somewhat surprising considering that Scott (2006) found that age was significant. Our lack of significance may be an effect of our small number of cases or a measurement error within the model, though the latter is less likely. In any event, theoretically speaking, the claim that age would have an effect on docket size was less convincing then any of our other arguments.

FURTHER DISCUSSION

Excepting that age was not significant, our findings that were significant offer an advance in the literature regarding the Supreme Court docket size. As we suggested, ideology is a significant factor in understanding points at which we can expect docket growth or, in this case, a diminishing docket size. Our findings are in line with earlier findings, which suggest that ideology plays a significant role in explaining judicial behavior as it pertains to decision making (Segal and Spaeth 1996; Segal and Cover 1989; Norpoth 1996). We can conclude from our research that ideology, again, is a significant indicator of, and does affect, the size of the docket. Furthermore, we can expect that, as the ideological composition on the Court changes, the docket size will also change.

Our veto finding adds new understanding to the dynamic relationship between the Court and the presidency. We know that the two branches have significant interactions with each other, but now we can also conclude that structural effects, such as vetoes, do in fact affect the Court's docket size. From the finding, we recommend that future research investigate the strategic interaction between the Court and the presidency as it relates to incidences of vetoing legislation that in fact may be unconstitutional. We conjecture that the presidency structurally acts as a "gate keeper" for legislation that is questionably constitutional. This evidence warrants further investigation of the power of judicial review and possibly the President's role in judicial review and the separation of powers (Bickel 1986).

Our ideological incongruence finding suggests similarity in the Court's institutional behavior in comparison to the presidency. As new presidents, especially with differing ideological tendencies from the previous administration, enter office, they tend to be more legislatively active than the previous administration (Moe 1985). We may be able to glean from our incongruence finding that similar behavior as it pertains to the Court and points of ideological incongruence can cause spikes in docket size.

CONCLUSION

In this chapter, we set out to explain the variance and causes of the shrinking United States Supreme Court docket. In doing so we uncovered some interesting and significant results; in particular, we confirmed the effect of the Court's mean ideology on docket size, along with the influence of presidential vetoes weeding out questionable or potentially challengeable legislation appearing on the Court's docket over time. Thereby, our findings yield explanatory significance regarding aggregate and institutional effects on docket size. However, future research should concentrate on understanding potential, individual effects that may constrain or shrink the docket size. Considering the consequence of the Court's rule of 4 when deciding its plenary docket, future research should examine anecdotal and individual strategic interactions between the justices to validate aggregate results. Such research ought to consider the Chief Justice's role in the certiorari process.

Though we are convinced that our aggregate findings yield significant explanatory power, an individual analysis will only help to strengthen our principle thesis that ideology is a significant factor in determining the Court's docket size.

BIBLIOGRAPHY

Bailey, Michael A., Brian Kamoie, and Forrest Maltzman. "Signals from the Tenth Justice: The Political Role of the Solicitor General in Supreme Court Decision Making." *American Journal of Political Science* 49, 1 (2005): 72–85.

Bickel, Alexander M. *The Least Dangerous Branch: The Supreme Court at the Bar of Politics*. 2nd ed. New Haven, CT: Yale University Press, 1986.

Caldeira, Gregory A., and John R. Wright. "Organized Interests and Agenda Setting in the U.S. Supreme Court." *The American Political Science Review* 82, 4 (1988): 1109–27.

Caldeira, Gregory A., and John R. Wright. "The Discuss List: Agenda Building in the Supreme Court." *Law & Society Review* 24, 3 (1990): 807–36.

Campbell, James E. "Cosponsoring Legislation in the U. S. Congress." *Legislative Studies Quarterly* 7, 3 (August 1982): 415–22.

Chemerinsky, Dean E. "The Incredible Shrinking Docket." *Trial*, March 1, 2007: 64–65.
Cordray, Margaret Meriwether, and Richard Cordray. "The Supreme Court's Plenary Docket." *Washington and Lee Law Review* 58, 3 (June 2001).
Duffy, Shannon P. "'Inside the Highest Court, Souter Describes Justices' Relationship, Caseload Trend." *Pennsylvania Law Weekly*, April 18, 1995: 10, 28.
Fenno, Richard. *Congressmen in Committees*. Boston: Little, Brown, 1973.
Greenhouse, Linda. "Dwindling Docket Mystifies Supreme Court." *The New York Times*, December 7, 2006.
Hellman, Arthur D. "The Shrunken Docket of the Rehnquist Court." *Supreme Court Review* 1996: 403–38.
Lane, Charles. "Caseload Reflects Court's Altered Role." *The Washington Post*, February 2, 2004: A15.
Lindquist, Stefanie A., David A. Yalof, and John A. Clark. "The Impact of Presidential Appointments to the U. S. Supreme Court: Cohesive and Divisive Voting Within Presidential Blocs." *Political Research Quarterly* 53, 4 (December 2000): 795–814.
McGuire, Kevin T. "Amici Curiae and Strategies for Gaining Access to the Supreme Court." *Political Research Quarterly* 47, 4 (December 1994): 821–37.
Mishler, William, and Reginald S. Sheehan. "The Supreme Court as a Countermajoritarian Institution? The Impact of Public Opinion on Supreme Court Decisions." *The American Political Science Review* 87, 1 (March 1993): 87–101.
Moe, Terry. "The Politicized Presidency." In *The New Direction in American Politics*, edited by John E. Chubb and Paul E. Peterson. Washington, DC: Brookings Institution Press, 1985.
Norpoth, Helmut. "Presidents and the Prospective Voter." *The Journal of Politics* 58, 3 (August 1996): 776–92.
O'Brien, David M. "A Diminished Plenary Docket – A Legacy of the Rehnquist Court." *Judicature* 89, 3 (2005): 134.
O'Brien, David M. "Join-3 Votes, the Rule of Four, the Cert. Pool, and the Supreme Court's Shrinking Plenary Docket." *Journal of Law & Politics* 13 (1997a): 779–808.
O'Brien, David M. "The Rehnquist Court's Shrinking Plenary Docket." *Judicature* 81 (1997b): 58–65.
Parker, Paul E. "Is a Lower Caseload the Same as a Lower Workload? Opinion Characteristics of the Burger and Rehnquist Courts." *The Justice System Journal* 20, 3 (1999): 299–316.
Perry, H. W. Jr. *Deciding to Decide: Agenda Setting in the United States Supreme Court*. Cambridge, MA: Harvard University Press, 1991.
Scott, Kevin M. "Shaping the Supreme Court's Federal Certiorari Docket." *The Justice System Journal* 27, 2 (2006): 191–207.
Segal, Jeffrey A., and Albert D. Cover. "Ideological Values and the Votes of U.S. Supreme Court Justices." *The American Political Science Review* 83, 2 (June 1989): 557–65.

Segal, Jeffrey A., and Cheryl D. Reedy. "The Supreme Court and Sex Discrimination: The Role of the Solicitor General." *The Western Political Quarterly* 41, 3 (September 1988): 553–68.

Segal, Jeffrey A., and Harold J. Spaeth. "The Influence of Stare Decisis on the Votes of United States Supreme Court Justices." *American Journal of Political Science* 40, 4 (November 1996): 971–1003.

Segal, Jeffrey A., Richard J. Timpone, and Robert M. Howard. "Buyer Beware? Presidential Success through Supreme Court Appointments." *Political Research Quarterly* 53, 3 (September 2000): 557–73.

Songer, Donald R. "Concern for Policy Outputs as a Cue for Supreme Court Decisions on Certiorari." *The Journal of Politics* 41, 4 (November 1979): 1185–94.

Songer, Donald R., Charles M. Cameron, and Jeffrey A. Segal. "An Empirical Test of the Rational Actor Theory of Litigation." *Journal of Politics* 57, 4 (1995): 1119–29.

Starr, Kenneth W. "The Supreme Court and Its Shrinking Docket: The Ghost of William Howard Taft." *Minnesota Law Review* 90 (2006): 1363–85.

Stevens, John Paul. "The Life Span of a Judge-Made Rule." *New York University Law Review* 58 (1983): 1–21.

Chapter 4

Judicial Retirements

SOME COMMENTS ON THE LITERATURE

Judicial death and retirement is an institutional factor of the U.S. Supreme Court which endures considerable scrutiny; from the competency of aging jurists to the notion of strategic retirements, many efforts have been made to understand the implications of the unavoidable aspects of lifetime tenure in circumstances of perpetual good behavior (Garrow 2000; Peppers and Oldfather 2011; Prakash 1999).

Among cynics, judicial deaths and retirements often constitute obvious evidence that the Court is merely another wellspring of political division and partisan squabbling;[1] Artemus Ward, a political scientist, argues that the generous retirement accommodations provoke justices to retire for partisan reasons, rather than in accordance with ailing mental health or infirmity: "generous retirement benefits coupled with a decreasing workload have reduced the departure process to partisan maneuvering" (Ward 2003). Chief Justice Burger, it is said, retired when he did so that President Reagan would be able to name his successor (Wermiel 1986); Justices Brennan and Marshall seemed to hold out for a Democratic victory in 1988 (Squire 1988). Yet, these views of the politicization of death and retirement are in the minority, and are not necessarily validated by the evidence and literature (Peppers and Oldfather 2011; Squire 1988).

Thus, despite a cynic's intuition that the retirement process would be overtly politicized, empirical evidence simply does not sustain such an intuition. Rather, it is much more likely to be the case that a Justice will remain on the Court until death or retire for pragmatic or personal reasons (Squire 1988; Zorn and Van Winkle 2000). Consider the case of Chief Justice Rehnquist who declines to retire, despite an opportunity which seemed politically opportune. Although the cynic might fault Rehnquist for not taking advantage of the political climate, Rehnquist was making decisions based on other, apolitical reasons. It was said that Rehnquist not only had a fondness for the Court and his integral role in its operations, but that he also had no fulfilling prospects outside of the Court which could compare to his continued service. It is not an enticing prospect for a lonely widower to forfeit a respectable job that he is confident he can continue to pursue (Obermayer 2009; Peppers and Oldfather 2011).

Examples of non-politicized reasons for retirement can include a minority status on the court, often represented in the number of dissents a Justice authors. Those who authored proportionally more dissents and found themselves in the minority were more likely to retire (Zorn and Van Winkle 2000). This conclusion seems to supersede a contrary finding (Squire 1988) which determined that Justices were less likely to retire from the Court when occupying the role of the minority opinion in an effort to resist changing Court policies and majority opinions.[2] Perhaps the most obvious reason motivating retirement is pension eligibility—the most overtly pragmatic reason available to a Justice. It goes without saying that pension eligibility raises the likelihood of retirement significantly (Gustman and Steinmeier 1986; Squire 1988; Stock and Wise 1990; Zorn and Van Winkle 2000).

It is not uncommon to see Justices serving past what is perceived to be their usefulness to justice and to the Court; empirical evidence shows us why this is the case: age and infirmity often have little impact on rates of retirement (Squire 1988; Zorn and Van Winkle 2000). Despite the fact that the duties required of a Justice may become difficult or impossible to perform in some instances, true to common knowledge about lifelong tenure, Justices often tend to hang on even though they seem to have outlived the ability to correctly perform their duties. It has been speculated that security in tenure itself is somewhat responsible for this behavior, and that it has even contributed to the lack of literature regarding lifelong tenure as a viable approach to the institutional structure of the Court.[3]

The cynic's intuitions about the politicization of judicial retirements are not well founded; analyses into the reasoning behind judicial retirements reveal the fact that the process of retirement is often a complex and personal matter for each Justice and does not seem to be particularly reliant on specific trends.

TIMING OF JUDICIAL RETIREMENT AND THE EFFECT OF IDEOLOGY ON RETIREMENT

The chapter seeks to answer the following questions: Do liberals serve on the bench longer than conservatives, or vice versa? What is the average age of retirement? Do conservatives serve on the bench longer than liberals? Are liberals more or less likely to die on the bench than conservatives? When judges plan on retiring, are they more likely to retire in the first or second term of a presidency? Are conservative judges more strategic about when to retire than liberal judges, or vice versa? All of these questions are important to answer because it will help to flesh out whether or not ideology is a significant factor in explaining judicial retirement. The hypothesis of this chapter is as follows: retiring from the bench is not a simple affair when a judge organically decides they are too old and must retire; rather, retiring on the bench is a function of politics, whereby justices are very aware of how their retirement could alter the ideological balance on the bench. Answering the aforementioned questions will help us to either confirm or deny this hypothesis.

Since 1789, 104 justices have died or retired from the Court. This finding indicates, on average, that there is a vacancy occurring every 26 months.[4] As President Carter can attest, there is no guarantee vacancy will occur this often. This is particularly true when a new jurist is joining a very evenly divided Court. Recent data shows that of all of the decisions the Supreme Court has rendered in the last 20 years, about 20 percent of them are decided in a 5–4 majority (Kuhn 2012).

Presidents take the nomination of a new Justice very seriously. Nominations to the bench are very important to presidents because they want to maintain their party's presence and preferred judicial outcomes on the bench. The first time this occurred was in the case of President John Adams and his infamous midnight appointments (Federal Judicial Center 1801). The federalists won the day with their nomination of Chief Justice Marshall; it is not too far-flung to suggest that the Constitution we have today should be titled "The Federal Constitution according to John Marshall." The legacy of the Federalist platform lives on today. As such, it seems reasonable that we surmise that judicial ideology matters, and thereby, that presidents must be cognizant of a Justice's ideology when nominating them.

We may safely assume that a president is, like any politician, a rational actor who wishes to achieve their policy goals, as well as those of their party. One method of advancing these goals is through the selection of justices to the Supreme Court. To maximize policy achievement, a president must be mindful of a jurist's ideological preferences before nomination and must consider who the jurist is replacing. During President Reagan's second term Chief Justice Burger retired. Reagan nominated, and had confirmed, Associate Justice Rehnquist, who was in fact even more conservative than Burger (see Table 4.5). In so doing, Reagan was able to increase the conservative presence on the bench, which meant Reagan's legacy would be more likely to be upheld over time. What is more is that Reagan nominated and had confirmed Justice Scalia who would come to be even more conservative than Rehnquist; Scalia served on the bench until nearly 12 years after the death of President Reagan until his own death in 2016.

In accordance with Article III of the Constitution, a justice may serve on the bench as long as they wish, so long as they maintain "good behavior."[5] As a consequence, justices on the highest Court in the land often serve for life.[6] Not all justices will die on the bench, of course.

Measuring a person's ideology is no easy task, though, political science makes reasonable attempts at doing so (Bailey 2012; Clark 2009; Ho and Quinn 2010; Woodruff 2014); of course, in science, there is no such thing as absolute precision. Therefore, in Table 4.1, we offer the best available measures of judicial ideology constructed by Segal and Cover (1989). These two scholars, using objective, external data—in particular editorial assessments of the justices prior to serving on the bench—began constructing a judicial ideology index in 1985. The table below offers judicial ideology scores ranging from 0, being a perfect conservative score, to 1 being a perfect liberal score. As you can see in the table, Justice Scalia received a perfect conservative score of 0, and Justice Marshall a perfect score of 1. Both judge's ideologies were measured not by votes cast, but rather by independent assessments of the judges prior to serving on the bench. The findings in Table 4.1 clearly confirm, based on the predictability of their vote patterns, that judges are ideological. It says first that their ideologies were measured without considering the votes they casted, but then includes them in the table; this is to show that their political leanings before taking office seem to be relevant in how they will rule. Moreover, how they *end up ruling in cases* reflects how they were *prior to* taking office and therefore reflects their ideology.

According to this data, we can say that liberal justices are likely to spend 3.5 to 5 years longer serving on the court than conservative justices. Before we draw any conclusions on these data, however, the next table shows the average age of retirement in accordance with ideology.

The list indicates that over the last 30 years, 10 justices have retired from the bench. The majority of the justices were right of center, but of course the degree and magnitude of their ideology varied. Many of the retiring justices had ideological scores ranging from .10 to .80, the most conservative to retire was Blackmun and the most liberal to retire was Marshall.

In Table 4.3 I measured the length of time the retiring justices were on the bench and considered their ideology. The table indicates that the 50 percent of the justices remained on the bench at least 30 years. The other 50 percent were Souter, O'Connor, Blackmun, Stewart, and Powell. Later in this chapter I provide case studies of each justice retiring from the bench to illustrate reasons and justifications for their retirement. The averages are conservative approximately 30 years on the bench, while liberals are about 27 years.

As stated earlier, all of the data analysis in this chapter only looks at the last ten justices retiring from the bench, as such, the following tables only include the data of the last ten Supreme Court justices to retire (case studies).

Table 4.1 Perceived Qualifications and Ideology of Supreme Court Nominees, 1937–2012. (Segal and Cover 1989)

Nominee	*Votes in Favor*	*Votes Opposed*	*Qualifications Score*	*Ideology Score*
Hugo O. Black	67	18	.160	.875
Stanley F. Reed	*		.875	.725
Felix Frankfurter	*		.965	.665
William O. Douglas	62	4	.820	.730
Frank Murphy	*		.650	1.000
Harlan F. Stone (CJ)	*		1.000	.300
James F. Byrnes	*		.800	.330
Robert H. Jackson	*		.915	1.000
Wiley B. Rutledge	*		1.000	1.000
Harold H. Burton	*		.930	.280
Fred M. Vinson (CJ)	*		.785	.750
Tom C. Clark	73	8	.125	.500
Sherman Minton	48	16	.355	.720
Earl Warren(CJ)	*		.855	.750
John M. Harlan	71	11	.750	.875
William J. Brennan, Jr.	*		1.000	1.000
Charles E. Whittaker	*		1.000	.500
Potter Stewart	70	17	1.000	.750
Byron White	*		.500	.500
Arthur J. Goldberg	*		.915	.750
Abe Fortas	*		1.000	1.000
Thurgood Marshall	69	11	.835	1.000
Abe Fortas (CJ)[a]	45	43	.635	.845
Warren E. Burger (CJ)	74	3	.960	.115
Clement Haynsworth, Jr.	45	55	.335	.160
G. Harrold Carswell	45	51	.111	.040
Harry A. Blackmun	94	0	.970	.115
Lewis F. Powell, Jr.	89	1	1.000	.165
William H. Rehnquist	68	26	.885	.045
John Paul Stevens	98	0	.960	.250
Sandra Day O'Connor	99	0	1.000	.415
William Rehnquist (CJ)	65	33	.400	.045
Antonin Scalia	98	0	1.000	.000
Robert H. Bork	42	58	.790	.095
Douglas Ginsburg[b]			.320	.000
Anthony Kennedy	97	0	.890	.365
David Souter	90	9	.765	.325
Clarence Thomas	52	48	.415	.160
Ruth Bader Ginsburg	96	3	1.000	.680
Stephen G. Breyer	87	9	.545	.475
John G. Roberts	78	22	.970	.120
Harriet E. Miers[c]			.360	.270
Samuel Alito	58	42	.810	.100

(Continued)

Table 4.1 (Continued)

Nominee	*Votes in Favor*	*Votes Opposed*	*Qualifications Score*	*Ideology Score*
Sonia Sotomayor	68	31	.810	.780
Elena Kagan	63	37	.730	.730

CJ = nominated for Chief Justice. * = voice vote; a = the vote on Fortas for the Chief Justice position was on cloture and failed to receive the necessary two-thirds majority; b = The Reagan Administration withdrew the nomination of Douglas Ginsburg; c = Harriet Miers withdrew her nomination.

The Qualifications Score ranges from 0 (least qualified) to 1 (most qualified); the Ideology Score ranges from 0 (most conservative) to 1 (most liberal). Data updated and backdated by Jeffrey Segal from Jeffrey Segal and Albert Cover, "Ideological Values and the Votes of Supreme Court Justices," *American Political Science Review* 83:557–565 (1989).

Indicated in table 1 is that the most conservative members on the Bench, over the last 80 years are: Justices Scalia, Alito, Rehnquist, and Thomas. In addition, the table includes nominees that were rejected and as indicated many of the justices rejected were very conservative, Bork and Carswell are very good examples. Their scores were close to a perfect 0 (or most conservative).

Table 4.2 List of Justices Retiring in the Last 30 Years, with Retirement Date and Ideology

Supreme Court Justice	*Year of Retirement*
John Paul Stevens	2010 (Liberal)
David Souter	2009 (Liberal)
Sandra Day O'Connor	2006 (Conservative)
William Rehnquist*	2005 (Conservative)
Harry Blackmun	1994 (Conservative)
Byron White	1993 (Liberal)
Thurgood Marshall	1991 (Liberal)
William J. Brennan, Jr.	1990 (Liberal)
Lewis F. Powell, Jr.	1987 (Conservative)
Potter Stewart	1981 (Conservative)

* Died on the court.
Source: Constructed and data compiled by Author using the Supreme Court Compendium.

Table 4.3 Length of Time in Office and Ideology

Supreme Court Justice	*Time on the Bench and Ideology*	*Age at Appointment*	*Age at Retirement (or Death)*
John Paul Stevens	34.50 yrs—Liberal	55	90
David Souter	18.33 yrs—Liberal	51	70
Sandra Day O'Connor	24.33 yrs—Moderate	51	76
William Rehnquist	33.68 yrs—Conservative	48	81 (died)
Harry Blackmun	24.17 yrs—Moderate	62	86
Byron White	31.22 yrs—Moderate	44	76
Thurgood Marshall	32.00 yrs—Liberal	59	83
William J. Brennan	33.78 yrs—Conservative	50	84
Potter Stewart	22.73 yrs—Conservative	43	66
Lewis F. Powell	15.48 yrs—Conservative	64	79

Table 4.4 Average Length of Time in Office, per Ideology, in Years

Ideology	*Average Time on the Bench*
Liberal Justices	29.93
Conservative Justices	25.08
Liberal Justices (Including Justice Blackmun)	28.78
Conservative Justices	25.26

Source: Constructed and data compiled by Author using the Supreme Court Compendium.

The numbers may change if EVERY Supreme Court justice to retire was analyzed, but including justices that served during a time when the definitions of "liberal" and "conservative" were changing would negate the point of this research.

When looking at the last ten Supreme Court Justices to retire, the average time spent serving is nearly a 5-year (4 years and 10 months) difference between liberal justices and conservative justices; conservative justices serve 4 years less than their liberal counterparts on average. This is strictly using the ABA ideology qualifications table. If we were to look at the same averages and place Justice Blackmun in the liberal category, then the difference in time spent in service is only slightly closer. What is very interesting about this finding is that justices serve on the bench for over a generation. If you consider, for a moment, justices serving for over 29 years, and often times the starting age for a judge is 58–62, then judges are on average leaving the bench at the extraordinary age of 80–85. This finding is important because as the nation relies on judges to decide serious social and moral issues, the composition of the Court is overwhelmingly stacked with elderly citizens from generations long past. It seems unreasonable for justices at that age to be able to properly relate to and understand social issues in the terms in which they are being fought; naturally, this isn't always the case, but it isn't an unfair generalization.

This table shows that conservative justices are about 2.5 years older than liberal justices when they retire from Supreme Court. It would seem, then, that if a conservative justice is 2.5 years older than a liberal justice, but spends nearly 5 years less time on the bench, then the trend is to nominate older conservative justices. A common-sense explanation for this could be that conservative justices have more legal and life experience by the time they are nominated, and are therefore more appealing to the often times left-leaning Senate. Further, this finding indicates that even though liberals stay

Table 4.5 Average Age of Retirement and Ideology

Ideology	*Average Age at Time of Retirement*
Liberal Justices	77.25
Conservative Justices	79.67

Table 4.6 The Effects of Ideology on the Timing or when a Judge Retires

Justice	*Ideology*	*Ideology of President at Time of Retirement*	*Term of President at Time of Retirement*
John Paul Stevens	Conservative	Liberal (Barack Obama)	1st
David Souter	Conservative	Liberal (Barack Obama)	1st
Sandra Day O'Connor	Conservative	Conservative (George W. Bush)	2nd
William Rhenquist	Conservative	Conservative (George W Bush)	2nd
Harry Blackmun	Conservative	Liberal (William Jefferson Clinton)	1st
Byron White	Moderate	Liberal (William Jefferson Clinton)	1st
Thurgood Marshall	Liberal	Conservative (George Bush Sr.)	1st
William J. Brennan Jr.	Liberal	Conservative (George Bush Sr.)	1st
Potter Stewart	Liberal	Conservative (Ronald Reagan)	1st
Lewis F. Powell	Conservative	Conservative (Ronald Reagan)	2nd

Source: Constructed and data compiled by Author using the Supreme Court Compendium.

on the bench longer, conservative justices are less likely to retire at a younger age, than their liberal counterparts. This finding does support the conventional wisdom that conservative judges tend to hold onto their seat longer.

In Table 4.5 we examine timing of retirement. Are conservative judges more likely to retire during a conservative presidency and likewise for liberals?

The interesting finding here is that the judges appear not to concern themselves so much about who is president at the time of their retirement. Both Marshall and Brennan retired during Bush Sr.'s term, and Justices Stevens and Souter retired during Obama's first term. This finding indicates that strategic retirement is overstated, confirming (Peppers and Oldfather 2011; Squire 1988); clearly these judges came to a point in their careers where they were just tired of being on the bench, whereas more ideological justices will likely not follow suit, for example, Ginsburg. In support of this conclusion about the Court, we have included the following brief case studies.

JUDICIAL CASE STUDIES: AN ANALYSIS OF THE LITERATURE ON THE ELEVEN MOST RECENT RETIRED OR LATE JUSTICES

These case studies bring together, where available, the explicit justification of the retiring or dying Justices as to why they either retired or stayed on the bench, as well as scholarly and media speculation as to the reasons for each Justice's retirement or decision to stay for life. Based on the following analysis, one can certainly conclude that judicial retirements are a politicized aspect of the institution of the Court. Yet, it appears to be one of the aspects which is least politicized, with many justices retiring primarily for personal or health reasons, rather than, or only partially, for reasons of political ideology and motivation. That said, some retirements are more partisan than others. As such, they constitute good evidence that the retirement process, while it can be politicized, is less political than some of the literature claims.

Antonin Scalia

Scalia's unexpected death in February of 2016 interferes with one's ability to judge whether or not Scalia was planning on retiring strategically such that his legacy as a judge and his political views would have more staying power. Was Scalia hoping for a more conservative president to retire or die under? This question is difficult to answer.

Interestingly, and quite distinctly from the other Justices which we investigate in this chapter, is that Scalia was asked this very question in no uncertain terms. On July 29, 2012, Fox News' Chris Wallace asked, "You're 76 years old; will you time your retirement so that a more conservative president can appoint a likeminded justice?" Scalia answered, "I don't know. I haven't decided when to retire." Wallace then pressed Scalia, suggesting that surely it went through his mind that he would not like to be replaced by someone with a contrary judicial philosophy. Scalia affirmed this, but he argued that no one, presumably if they cared about their work on the Court, would want to see everything they worked undone by their replacement—"unless you think I am a fool," he concluded with a chuckle.[7] It seems fair that one wouldn't want all of their work to be undone by an ideological opponent, but it doesn't follow from this that Scalia timed his retirement to coincide with a more conservative President.

Of the testimony from Scalia regarding his retirement, what stands out is that he considered his enjoyment of the job and his ability to perform it properly to be two necessary components of his continued service. Should these diminish or go away, it would seem that Scalia would retire. During a lecture at the University of Minnesota Law School, Scalia stated that "[a]s soon as I think I'm getting lazier and I just can't do the job as well, I'm going to get off there. I want to preserve whatever reputation I have," he added that, "[i]f you've lost your smarts, yeah you should get off. But that hasn't been the case."[8] In an article for Forbes by Richard Harris, Scalia is said to have remarked about retirement that, "I love my job. If I didn't love it, I wouldn't do it any longer" noting that he could have easily retired at 65 with full pay and benefits if he has wanted to.[9] In an extended, two-part interview with

Jennifer Senior, Scalia was asked how he would know "when it's time to go?" "When I'm not hitting on all eight cylinders" he responded matter-of-factly. Senior pressed him a bit further asking what a telltale sign might be or look like. Scalia offered the following:

> One will be that I won't enjoy it as much as I do. I think that's the beginning of the end. I was worried lately about the fact that the job seems easier. That I really don't have to put in the excessively long hours that I used to. I still work hard. But it does seem easier than it used to. And that worried me. You know: *Maybe I'm getting lazy.* You know, I'm not doing it as thoroughly, or whatever. But after due reflection, I've decided the reason it's getting easier is because so many of the cases that come before us present the issue of whether we should extend one of the opinions from the previous 27 years that I've been here, which I dissented from in the first place![10]

Although Scalia is unabashedly a conservative both in his politics and in his judicial philosophy, it does not seem plausible to suggest that Scalia was attempting to wait for a more conservative justice in order that he could retire in ideological safety. Any aspirations Scalia had for political expediency were secondary to his guiding principles; journalist Peter Hitchens once asked Scalia if "he was ever tempted to abandon Strict Construction and interpret the constitution in a conservative way, to match his liberal opponents." Scalia responded that, although he was sure that "it would be fun for a while" his real aim was to "restore the idea that law was law, and Judges interpreted it according to law."[11] Despite the fact that Scalia acknowledged that he would not like to see all of his work undone by an ideological opponent, the ever candid and controversial Scalia did not assent to the proposition that he would strategize with his own retirement, something which would not seem to be anything controversial to such a figure, and therefore easily admissible. Given that Justice Scalia really liked his job and had not lost any of his faculties, the likelihood of him retiring was very small. Moreover, since Scalia's death was unanticipated, there does not seem to be any sense in which Scalia intended to hang onto his position on the Court for as long as possible such that a Republican might nominate someone to replace him, rather than President Obama.

John Paul Stevens

Justice Stevens is an interesting case when trying to understand the timing of a Justice's retirement. Stevens was originally appointed by the Republican president Gerald Ford, and it does not appear that Stevens retired at a time that would guarantee that his spot on the bench would be filled by a conservative justice; indeed, Stevens himself had a rather liberal streak as his career progressed, and often found himself dissenting against opinions penned by the likes of Scalia. So what might have prompted Stevens to retire when he did? The answer may lie in *Bush v. Gore*. In the case that ultimately decided the victory of the 2000 presidential election, Justice Stevens wrote a dissent that could explain (at least partially) the timing of his retirement. The following excerpt from Stevens' opinion sums up nicely his disdain for the majority's decision:

> What must underlie petitioners' entire federal assault on the Florida election procedures is an unstated lack of confidence in the impartiality and capacity of the state judges who would make the critical decisions if the vote were to proceed. Otherwise, their position is wholly without merit. The endorsement of that decision by the majority of this Court can only lend credence to the most cynical appraisal of the work of judges throughout the land. It is confidence in the men and women who administer the judicial system that is the true backbone of the rule of law. Time will one day heal the wound to that confidence that will be inflicted by today's decision. One thing, however, is certain. Although we may never know with complete certainty the identity of the winner of this year's presidential election, the identity of the loser is perfectly clear. It is the Nation's confidence in the judge as an impartial guardian of the rule of law.[12]

This case is a bit of a sore spot for the fiercest defenders of Textualism and conservative judicial interpretation. *Bush v. Gore* was a Catch-22 that stumped even the staunchest conservative judges on High Court. It is argued that if the Justices were to have strictly reviewed the law, it would have likely guaranteed the victory of the liberal candidate for the presidency, Al Gore. Conservative judges did not allow that to happen, though, and in a 5–4 decision, ensured George W. Bush became the 43rd President of the United States.

Justice Stevens adamantly opposed the majority's opinion, as shown in the excerpt above. Perhaps this was part of his decision to retire soon after George W. Bush left office. Justice Stevens may have not wanted a president who did not win, in his mind, in a legitimate way, to nominate a justice to fill his position on the bench. Respect for not merely the person in the Oval Office, but how they arrived there, may have been more to the forefront of Justice Stevens' mind during his retirement than political party or ideological congruence. At the time that Justice Stevens retired, the Senate was firmly controlled by the Democrats, which would have made it *very* unlikely for a conservative justice to replace him, considering President Obama was also in office at the time. If Justice Stevens had an ideological change of heart during his time on the bench, or if he felt the politics of the republicans left him behind, then this would have been an ideal time for him to retire given the political makeup of the legislative and executive branches, especially considering his old age. Indeed, this is precisely what Professor of Criminal Justice, Christopher E. Smith, suggests,

> Thus Stevens's moderate wing of the Republican Party was nearly extinct by the final two decades of his career on the Court. It was no surprise then that he, [. . .] timed his retirement to permit a Democratic president, Barack Obama, to select his replacement.[13]

Smith bases his conclusion on Stevens' distinguished career of protecting, among other rights, prisoners' rights and the rights of the accused—something missing from republican ideology during the time that he retired. If what Smith writes is accurate, it is plausible on its face that his retirement was politically motivated. On the other hand, if he was still a relatively republican or conservative person, as he seemed to be when Ford appointed him, he may not have been politically motivated to retire under Obama, and instead retired due to his age of 90 years. Perhaps an in depth analysis of Justice Stevens' political ideology would yield a clearer result as to his retirement, but the evidence does seem to *lean* in favor of his retirement being politically motivated.

David Souter

President George H. W. Bush made a strategic move in nominating Justice Souter to the Supreme Court, but Justice Souter may not have strategized his retirement for any outcome other than returning home. It was common knowledge how much he loved his home state of New Hampshire, and he never minced words when speaking about how much he disliked Washington, D.C. However, this could also be explained by noting that, over time, Justice Souter came to vote reliably with his liberal colleagues—making things, in the end, a poor investment from a conservative point of view.[14]

After Justice David Souter retired, he said that he, "drove north from Washington with no regrets about the prior nineteen years or about the decision to try living a normal life for whatever time might remain."[15] Satisfied with his service to his country, Souter wished to return home to enjoy the remainder of his life—specifically before he was too aged to mountain climb, as he loved to do.[16] As was the case with Justice Stevens, it is difficult to ascertain the motives behind Justice Souter's retirement. Souter did not make any overt comments about his desire to retire under an ideologically congruent President or Senate, though his liberal leanings would line up best with his retirement under Obama, especially since Obama enjoyed a strong Democrat majority in the Senate during his first 2 years. Perhaps an analysis of Souter's political ideology would yield something more conclusive, but there is some evidence that Souter intended to retire under a democratic president. Specifically, he was thought to intend to retire after 15 years on the Court when he would be eligible for retirement at full salary,[17] and since he specifically waited for the Democratic President Obama, it makes sense that, given his political views, which were at the time of his retirement more in keeping with the left than the right, he would retire under a Democrat if he could; indeed, Smith suggests the same or similar motivation for both Souter and Stevens.[18] Such a suggestion is also corroborated by Totenberg, who wrote that

> Factors in his decision no doubt include the election of President Obama, who would be more likely to appoint a successor attuned to the principles Souter has followed as a moderate-to-liberal member of the court's more liberal bloc over the past two decades.[19]

Sandra Day O'Connor

Justice O'Connor retired in 2006 in the middle of President Bush's two terms in office and represents an example of ideological congruence; though it is important to note whether or not this is significant or coincidental. In 2000, Sandra Day O'Connor and her husband, John, were attending a dinner party on election night; the race was extremely close between George W. Bush and Al Gore. Toward the closing of the vote counting, it seemed clear that Gore had edged out Bush as the President of the United States. Several individuals who were at the dinner party, as reported in numerous publications from the *Weekly Standard* to the *Wall Street Journal*, indicated that O'Connor was visibly upset over the apparent Democrat victory in Florida, and that she and her husband bemoaned having to wait another 4 years or more before she could retire; O'Connor apparently did not want to retire under a Democrat president given the likelihood of her replacement being ideologically incongruous.[20] This seems to evidence the notion that O'Connor's retirement was strategic and political, thereby differentiating herself from Justices Souter and Stevens, who did not display such commitment to a particular party. O'Connor's activities within the Republican Party itself may have also contributed to this loyalty. As a result, O'Connor's impartiality and honor have been questioned due to her decision and stance in *Bush v. Gore*, ultimately siding with Bush on the matter.[21] As Bush won the presidency—and for two terms—ultimately, O'Connor was able to retire during an administration she agreed with ideologically. As it so happens, the Senate was under its strongest Republican control during the entirety of Bush's administration, making retirement all the more tempting and reasonable, assuming her motivations were indeed political; convenient for her, too, considering she retired in large part to provide her husband (diagnosed with Alzheimer's) with the proper care necessary to ease the rest of his life. While it is not set in stone that O'Connor retired for political reasons, there is certainly evidence to suggest that she did, and if so, then her strategy worked out quite well, since she was replaced with the highly conservative Samuel Alito. It is worth noting that she didn't retire during Bush's first term and risked another election before retiring; it is not clear precisely what this means in the broader context of her retirement.

William Rehnquist

Of all the case studies in this chapter, Chief Justice Rehnquist is the only other justice besides Justice Scalia who died while still serving on the Supreme Court. The lifelong tenure guaranteed by the Constitution[22] was intended to ensure that Supreme Court Justices were independent from ideological pressures so often found in the other two branches of government due to electoral politics. However, as we have seen so far with Justice O'Connor, this is not always the case.

As Chief Justice, Rehnquist voted conservatively throughout his career and was often a "lone dissenter" when it came to cases in which he had a conservative interest; his behavior on the bench was quite distinct from Souter and Stevens, and even O'Connor to an extent. Rehnquist was also another example in the history of the Court of the "good behavior" clause in the Constitution seemingly backfiring; he missed many hearings while he was sick in the last years of his life.[23] He died in 2005 during the second term of a conservative president, George W. Bush. Although Rehnquist was a very partisan Justice, the fact that he could have safely retired in the early years of President Bush's presidency seems to indicate that his death on the bench was motivated by at least one of two things, if not both. First, he thought it reasonable he would die on the Court during one of Bush's terms, and therefore, loving or enjoying the Court, need not retire, even in poor health; second, he was indifferent to the ideology of his replacement, given Bush could have lost his second run for the presidency, leaving Rehnquist either to retire or die under a Democrat president. Although there was speculation by the media[24] that Rehnquist wanted to wait to retire under a conservative president, Rehnquist had already lost his wife, Nan in 1991; it therefore seems reasonable to assume that his service on the Court was his primary focus given that he did not retire during Bush's first term. Moreover, Rehnquist, during some other speculation over his retirement due to his failing health, made it clear that he has no intention of retiring, stating that, "I want to put to rest the speculation and unfounded rumors of my imminent retirement. I am not about to announce my retirement. I will continue to perform my duties as chief justice as long as my health permits."[25] Prima facie, Rehnquist's death on the Court would not seem to be ideologically motivated.

Harry Blackmun

Harry Blackmun was, at the time of his appointment to the Court, moderately right leaning; however, by the end of his tenure as a Justice, he often voted with the liberal wing of the Court. Given his ideological bent at the time of his retirement, is it reasonable to propose that Blackmun's retirement in 1994 was strategic? His apparent convictions, his own personal testimony, the testimony of others, and his own decisions on the bench seem to depict that his retirement was not motivated by ideology. Linda Greenhouse wrote in a piece for the *New York Times* that "It has been Justice Blackmun's approach to deciding cases, rather than any ideological commitment, that appears to account for his evolution as a judicial liberal." This is confirmed when she quoted Georgetown Law Professor, Chai Feldblum, someone who had clerked for Justice Blackmun; Professor Feldblum noted, "He came with certain guiding lights that are just embedded in his personality, and they never changed."[26] Blackmun himself noted, musing to Justice Stevens, that "neither of us has changed; the Court has changed under us." Though he qualified it by saying, "How much truth there is to that, I don't know." What can be concluded, however, is that he did not consider himself a man primarily motivated by partisan ideology. Blackmun, further, did not retire upon democratic President Clinton's election due to Justice White's retirement that year;[27] it is worth remarking that, at the time that Blackmun was considering retirement, during both the 102nd and 103rd Congress, there was a strong Democrat presence.[28] Professor of Political Science, Tinsley Yarbrough, suggests that Blackmun's departure was, at least in part, politically motivated, writing

> advancing age and the election of Bill Clinton, a president committed to abortion rights, had convinced him that the 1993 term would be his last on the bench.[29]Blackmun also made no secret of his elation at Clinton's election and thus, presumably, his willingness to put the naming of his successor in the new president's hands.[30]

Segal and Epstein, citing Ward and DiTullio and Schochet, claim that "[w]anting to ensure that his replacement would also be a liberal, [Blackmun] waited until a Democrat won the presidency."[31] Segal and Epstein seem to be referring to this passage in Ward, where Ward writes, "Blackmun's remarks prior to the election of Democrat Bill Clinton and his actions following the election clearly demonstrate that partisanship was part of his equation."[32] They might also be referring to DiTullio and Schochet when they wrote

> Both men had previously made clear their desire to retire, and both had subtly let it be known that they wished to leave the Court during a Democratic administration.[33] [. . .] In Justice Blackmun's case, although nominated by President

> Richard Nixon, the Justice had grown considerably more liberal over the course of his tenure on the Court, and he wanted to ensure that his seat remained in the hands of someone ideologically like-minded.[34] [. . .] In addition, all three retirements from the Court since Professor Ross published his article in 1990—Justices Marshall, Blackmun, and White—have been stamped by some level of partisan considerations.[35]

However, DiTullio and Schochet also refer to Ward, and Ward's claim that Blackmun made remarks about wishing to retire under a Democrat president are not strong enough evidence to conclude that his motivation for retirement was entirely political—though with the testimony of Yarbrough above, such corroboration may give credence to the notion that Blackmun retired for somewhat political reasons. Indeed, another reason to believe this is that, unlike many other justices, Justice Blackmun was not forced to step down due to health concerns.[36] While it is not *conclusive* that Blackmun retired for political reasons, it is not farfetched to suppose that they played *some* role in his retirement.

Byron White

Given Justice White's voting record, which often shifted as far to the left as it did to the right,[37] it is difficult to discern whether his retirement from the court in 1993 under President Clinton was motivated by a desire to do right by any particular party or ideology. This is important because White's retirement allowed for President Clinton to nominate Justice Ruth Bader Ginsburg, generally accepted as one of the most liberal judges on the court, as White's successor. White's status as the last justice nominated by a Democratic president to often (enough) vote with conservatives serves as a strong testament to the non-partisan attitude he held toward the position. As Justice Stevens noted regarding Justice White

> At the time of his appointment, Byron responded to press inquiries about his judicial philosophy by succinctly stating that his job was 'to decide cases.' One of the reasons why he was such a great judge is that he did not have an agenda that he sought to achieve through his decisions. He took the cases one at a time, deciding each on the basis of an impartial and intelligent study of the relevant facts and law.[38]

Despite this testimony, it has been suggested that White's retirement was strategic. This claim seems to come from an article in the *Washington Post*, written by Joan Biskupic which claimed that, according to Ward

> Biskupic [. . .] wrote that White "apparently is considering stepping down." Though she cited no sources for her information, she reported that White "has

said that since he came in with a Democratic administration, it would be fitting to retire under a Democratic administration."[39]

This claim was repeated by DiTullio and Schochet who wrote

> Both [Justices Blackmun and White] had previously made clear their desire to retire, and both had subtly let it be known that they wished to leave the Court during a Democratic administration.[40]

DiTullio and Schochet also claim that

> In addition, all three retirements from the Court since Professor Ross published his article in 1990—Justices Marshall, Blackmun, and White—have been stamped by some level of partisan considerations.[41]

Ward collaborates this, noting that

> Based on the timing, their relatively good health, or both, Justices Harlan, Stewart, Burger, White, and Blackmun can be classified as being motivated by partisanship in their departure decisions.[42]

Yet, these accounts are not sufficiently substantiated; either the sourceless article from the *Washington Post* from Biskupic is cited, or the claims concerning White's political motivations is left unsubstantiated; indeed, Ward notes that "there is little direct evidence to substantiate such a conclusion" *even though* he then proceeds to suggest White's retirement was motivated by partisanship. Segal and Epstein also make this claim ("[White] had long said he wanted to leave the bench when a Democrat occupied the White House") despite providing no evidence.[43] Perhaps the best piece of evidence that one can give is that White retired at a time in Clinton's presidency when the Senate was safely held by a Democrat majority, but this could be incidental.

Given White's own record in his opinions, as well as the perception of him held by his contemporaries, it would appear that White's retirement from the Supreme Court was not motivated by political maneuvering or party allegiance, but rather pure self-interest. Indeed, around the time of his retirement, he modestly remarked that "someone else should be permitted to have a like experience."[44] If there was substantial partisanship at play, the evidence of it has not yet been uncovered.

Thurgood Marshall

At the time of Thurgood Marshall's retirement in 1991, the Court had become overwhelmingly conservative, with Marshall serving as the one of the Court's last bastions of progressive thinking. The departure of Marshall's confidant and friend, Justice William J. Brennan, only exacerbated his displeasure with the 1991 arrangement of the Court. After Brennan's departure and the ideological change of the court, Justice Marshall issued a remarkable number of dissenting opinions—especially compared to when he first arrived on, at the time, a more liberal Court.[45] Additionally, Marshall was on record making numerous disparaging comments on the state of affairs publicly, noting in one of his final dissents (during a death penalty case) that "Power, not reason, is the new currency of this court's decision making."[46]

Marshall serves as an example of a justice who, if health permitted, would have strategized his retirement; indeed, according to Ward, he did strategize his retirement as long as he could.[47] Indeed, Juan Williams writes that "[t]he justice told friends he no longer thought he could stay on the Court until Democrats regained control of the White House."[48] Yet, despite this apparent politicization, Marshall did not act entirely strategically. Marshall was already feeling the effects of ailing health, when Jimmy Carter was still president and could have replaced him with a like-minded judge, and was even approached by officials in Carter's administration who were prompting him to retire once it was obvious that Raegan would take the White House.[49] So, if having someone of his ideological stamp replace him was his top priority, he could have simply retired then and been done with it. Moreover, if Marshall was entirely ideologically driven, he could have attempted to hold out for a Democrat replacement to President Bush Sr. (which would have come to pass) by waiting on the Court longer than he did, failing health and all, in the same way that Rehnquist held on for too long in the years to come. As it so happens, Marshall died in 1993 during the democratic President Clinton, so such a plan would actually have worked, though it would have done the Court some measure of harm in the same manner that having an infirm—both mentally and physically—justice tends to do. While it may be the case that Marshall's retirement was in part politically motivated, it was clearly not strong enough to be of overriding importance to the justice—at least not at the time he *could have* retired. It may have been quite strong at the time that he *did* retire, though he felt as though he could not affect his strategic goals.

William J. Brennan, Jr.

Brennan, like his peer and friend on the bench, Justice Marshall, was a consistently liberal judge; his perfect 1.0 score on the "Perceived Qualifications and Ideology of Supreme Court Nominees, 1937–2012" table (Table 4.5) attests to his liberal passions. Brennan's career, as is the case with some justices, ended due to severe health issues; in his case, he suffered a second stroke in 1990, forcing his hand on the issue of retirement. It would seem that, were Brennan truly motivated by ideology, he would likely have held out the additional 2 years in the hopes of President Bush Sr. being replaced by a Democrat—or, perhaps dying on the Court to give Bush Sr. less time to secure a successful nomination. However, this may not have been the case, since justices are also very much concerned with their ability to complete their jobs and functions on the bench; if Brennan were to be completely incapacitated, or completely unable to work due to health reasons, as would eventually happen to Chief Justice Rehnquist, he would seem to betray something much more fundamental about his position on the Court than simply retiring in a politically strategic way. DiTullio and Schochet, citing Ward, argue that Brennan did not want to have a justice nominated by a Republican president fill his seat on the Court

> With respect to Justice Brennan, for example, the former Justice made no secret in his years after leaving the Court that he regretted having retired under a Republican president. Justice Brennan felt that he should have remained on the Court longer and waited, despite his failing health, for a Democrat to take back the White House.[50]

Ward does argue as much, but not in the sections of the book cited by DiTullio and Schochet (pp. 202–3), and does not make claims as strong as those just noted, writing:

> While only nine of nineteen departed under copartisan presidents—presidents who shared their party affiliation, general ideological outlook, or both—nearly all the rest exhibited other forms of partisanship, like attempting to hang on to their seats until a favorable administration took office. This was certainly the case for such justices as William O. Douglas and Thurgood Marshall, and probably the case for Hugo Black and William J. Brennan.[51]

Segal and Epstein note that "A stroke forced the liberal Brennan to leave the bench. Otherwise he 'had no intention' of retiring during George H. W. Bush's presidency"[52] which certainly *insinuates* that Brennan had no intention of retiring specifically under Bush *because* it was Bush, a Republican President—especially given this portion of the book in question. However, as far as we can tell, when Justice Brennan is quoted as saying he "had no intention" of retiring, he did so in the context of his health, not in the context of an administration presumed to be wholly disagreeable to him.[53] Given Brennan's stature and work ethic, as well as his regrets about leaving the Court when he did, it can be inferred that, had conditions allowed, he would have seen his time as a Justice through to the very end, and not for any explicitly politically motivated reasons.[54]

Lewis F. Powell

Powell's retirement at the age of 79 in 1987, following a 15-year-long career, is famous for sparking an intense confirmation battle for President Reagan, whose first two appointees were rejected.[55] Any perceived party loyalty on the part of Powell is difficult to determine, especially considering that he was often a thorn in the side of conservatives in rulings like *Roe v. Wade*, as well as in cases in which he voted contrary to conservative interests on matters of affirmative action and the separation of church and state.[56]

Despite self-identifying as a Democrat, evidence suggests he was quite conservative, and his retirement allowed for a conservative president the opportunity to appoint who he saw fit. Powell was convinced to stay on the Court, rather than retiring in the early '80s, by his family, leading to a later retirement in 1987 citing failing health.[57] Had he retired in the early 1980s, he would have knowingly been retiring under a Republican-controlled Senate, making President Reagan's task in determining a successor and getting them successfully instated significantly easier than if the political climate changed—which it did. In 1987 the Democrats had a strong majority in the Senate.[58] Powell's decision to retire, though it seems to be the most strongly founded in concerns about his health and ability to continue as vigorously with his work as he once had, was almost certainly influenced by politics. This is so since he was interested in seeing President Reagan nominated another judge during his tenure as President, having already nominated Justice O'Connor, someone who Powell very much approved of. Powell, both during his thoughts about retirement in the early 1980s during Reagan's first term, and again in the mid- to late 1980s during Reagan's second term, were partially motivated by the worry that a Democrat would see the White House. So, while Powell's decision to retire was influenced by many factors, some political and some apolitical, these interests did still affect his final decision, it would seem, and is another instance of politicization and political strategizing during the retirement stage of the institution of the Court.[59]

Potter Stewart

Stewart's retirement at the young (for a Supreme Court Justice) age of 66, in 1981, was motivated primarily by familial concerns, with a *Washington Post* obituary noting that he had wished to spend more time with his grandchildren. The obituary goes on to note that Justice Stewart was resolutely non-partisan in his judicial approach and aims, noting that, when asked about political ideology, Stewart replied "I have enough difficulty understanding what those words mean even in the field of political life.

And I find it impossible to know what those words mean when carried over into the judicial work." He, furthermore, encouraged the abandonment of ideology as a foremost duty of any judge, noting that those who did not thought themselves to be "philosopher kings."[60] Given this information and Justice Stewart's voting record, which was rather liberal, as was his general ideology (Justice Stewart's ideology score was .750), it seems unreasonable to suggest that his retirement under President Reagan was ideologically motivated. Segal and Epstein, as well as Ward suggest that the retirement might have been politically motivated; however, as Ward admits, "there is no direct evidence that partisanship motivated him," and such claims appear to be purely speculative.[61]

REMARKS CONCERNING THE FINDINGS OF THE CASE STUDIES

Of the deaths and retirement decisions analyzed above, it seems reasonable to say that just a little over half of those surveyed for analysis (Justices: O'Connor, Powell, Blackmun, Souter, Marshall, and Stevens) at least considered, and very likely were influenced by, the political ramifications of the timing of their retirement in their decision to retire from the Court; O'Connor might be one of the most obvious examples of this, given the reports of her dissatisfaction at the possibility of Vice President Gore winning the 2000 election. This is, of course, not to say that this was their *primary reason* for retiring when they did, only that it may have informed or influenced their decision making process, indicating that they have political interests bound up with the timing of their retirement. Just under half of the Justices (Stewart, Brennan, White, Rehnquist, and Scalia) seem either to have hidden their political motivations for retirement rather well, or simply did not bother to consider the political ramifications of their retirement at a given time.

So, while there is certainly some measure of politicization in the retirement aspect of the goings on of the Court, it is not overtly or consistently politicized—quite unlike the process of nominating and confirming justices.

CONCLUSION AND PREDICTIONS

This chapter aimed to answer the questions posed at its outset and to examine the effects of ideology on judicial retirements. Judges tend to stay on the bench for a very long time, regardless of ideology—though conservatives tend to outdo liberals in this regard. Often, judges are not strategically

Table 4.7 Forecast of Judicial Retirements in the Years to Come

Supreme Court Justice	*Political Ideology*	*Year Appointed to Supreme Court*	*Predicted Date of Retirement*
(CJ) John G. Roberts	Conservative	September 2005	December 2031
Anthony M. Kennedy	Conservative	February 1988	January 2019
Clarence Thomas	Conservative	October 1991	January 2027
Ruth Bader Ginsburg	Liberal	August,1993	May 2022
Stephen G. Breyer	Liberal	August 1994	May 2023
Samuel Alito, Jr.	Conservative	January 2006	May 2034
Sonia Sotomayor	Liberal	August 2009	May 2038
Elena Kegan	Liberal	August 2010	May 2039

retiring; rather, they leave when they think life calls them to leave, for example, Justice Souter (Baker and Zeleny 2009). As outlined in the brief literature review which opened this chapter, personal decisions, by a process of elimination (and after retirement benefits eligibility), are both the most likely reasons, and yet the most difficult reason to quantify, for a justice leaving the Court. Even still, timing does indicate that judicial retirements *can* be politically motivated. For example, Justice O'Connor's retirement during the first term of President Bush indicated a very strategic retirement to replace a moderate conservative member with what she hoped would be an ideologically congruent successor.[62]

Using this sort of information to predict and anticipate retirements is the next step. The data in this chapter indicates that conservatives will stay on the bench for a shorter period of time than liberals, but likely retire once they cross the age of 80, with the maximum amount of years spent on the bench by a Conservative being just shy of 26 years.

The next table is the current (2014) U.S. Supreme Court. Data included in this table is a justice's ideology, year appointed to the Court, and predicted date of retirement according to their ideology.

Using the data from this analysis we find that Justice Kennedy should retire in 2019. Justice Scalia died in 2018 and his seat was replaced with Neil Gorsuch. He would be expected to retire in 27 years. Justice Kennedy retired in August 2018 and was replaced with Brett Kavanaugh. He is likely to retire in 29 years. Both are very conservative and likely will serve on the Court till their 80s. The most ailing Justice on the Court is Ruth Beta Ginsburg in her 80s she would likely retire if the presidency is won by a liberal candidate in 2020. However, if President Trump is reelected the chances of her surviving the second term are not optimal, which could give President Trump another significant appointment to the bench. In all, we do not expect any retirements anytime soon. Of course, death is something no one can predict, but we think are retirement guide and measurements are fairly accurate. Expect big changes in the Court in the early 2020s.

NOTES

1. As Winkle and Zorn note, "There is ample anecdotal evidence that political factors are influential in justices' retirement decisions"; see Winkle and Zorn (2000, 149–50).

2. Though Squire notes that opportunities to issue opinions and dissents has increased over time (see note 8); if such a trend has continued, Zorn and Van Winkler's study may reveal a recent change in the mechanics of the Court.

3. "Professors might be thought part of a conspiracy of silence regarding life tenure. We favor life tenure so much for ourselves that we are unwilling to confront its drawbacks for judges. Indeed, no one should doubt that the conventional wisdom regarding life tenure is quite strong. In rather bulky and recent law reviews dedicated to 'Judicial Independence and Accountability,' no academic seriously questioned whether life tenure serves any purpose. Instead, most assumed the value of life tenure and noted its tension with accountability" (Prakash 1999).

4. See Wikipedia Contributors (2015) for quick reference; see The Supreme Court Historical Society (n.d.) for more specific details.

5. See Article III, section 1 of the United States Constitution.

6. Of the Justices which have served on the Court, 50 have died on the Court and 54 have either resigned or retired. It was much more common in the earlier days of the United States for a justice to die on the Bench than it is in contemporary times.

7. See Scalia (2012).

8. See Bakst (2015).

9. See Harris (2016).

10. See Scalia, In Conversation: Antonin Scalia (2013).

11. See Hitchens (2016).

12. Justice Stevens dissenting in *Bush v. Gore*, 531 U.S. 98, 148 L. Ed. 2d 388, 121 S. Ct. 525 (2000).

13. Smith (2015, 10).

14. See Baker and Zeleny (2009); Souter became markedly less conservative over time, and his replacement by a liberal wouldn't thereby change the balance of the Court.

15. As quoted in V (2011), originally from Souter's fiftieth-reunion class report.

16. See Baker and Zeleny (2009).

17. Yarbough (2005, 258).

18. Smith (2015, 10).

19. See Totenberg (2009).

20. See pages 375–78 in Neumann (2003); both O'Connor's behavior, as well as testimony from her husband confirm the notion that she was upset by Gore's apparent victory, thereby reinforcing the idea of a strategic retirement.

21. Ibid. The impartiality of the Justices of the court has been questioned in the wake of *Bush v. Gore*, including that of Justice O'Connor.

22. See Article III, section 1 of the United States Constitution.

23. See Wrightsman (2008, 91). Rehnquist, due to thyroid cancer, missed over 40 oral arguments in 2004.

24. See Neumann (2003, 378).

25. See Johns and Mears (2005).
26. See Greenhouse (1994).
27. See Ward (2003, 208).
28. See Wikipedia contributors (2015), "102nd United States Congress," for quick reference; based on the data compiled by the Senate Historical Office (2015). See also the entry for the 103rd Congress.
29. Yarbrough (2008, 318).
30. Ibid., 323.
31. (2005, 40).
32. (2003, 209).
33. (2004, 1103).
34. Ibid., 1104.
35. Ibid., 1109.
36. Ward (2003, 208).
37. See Schwartz (1995, 273). In addition to the aforementioned quotation, Schwartz notes that "[White] went his own way, voting against the Chief just as often as not."
38. See Stevens (2013, 907). This article is of the lecture Stevens gave at the University of Colorado.
39. Ward (2003, 207); this claim was reiterated by DiTullio and Schochet (2004, 1103, 1104 fn. 40) who cited Biskupic.
40. DiTullio and Schochet (2004, 1103).
41. Ibid., 1109; DiTullio and Schochet cite Ward (2003, 209–10) on this point.
42. Ward (2003, 209).
43. Segal and Epstein (2005, 40); we are not sure, but this claim might *also* derive from Biskupic's article.
44. See Biskupic (2002).
45. Ibid.
46. Quoted in Rosenthal (1991).
47. Ward (2003, 19–20).
48. Williams (1998, 391).
49. Ward (2003, 203–6); Williams (1998, Ch. 31).
50. (1109).
51. Ward (2003, 154); this notion is once again suggested on p. 177 by Ward, but so far as we can tell no evidence is ever adduced to evince this point.
52. Segal and Epstein (2005, 39).
53. Time Wire Services (1990).
54. Ward (2003, 202); "When Justice White asked for advice on the retirement decision in March 1993, Brennan told him not to leave, and added that it was the worst decision he had ever made."
55. See Biskupic and Barbash (1998); final section.
56. See Kamen (1987) for additional details.
57. Ibid.
58. See Wikipedia contributors (2015), both "97th United States Congress" and "100th United States Congress," for quick reference; based on the data compiled by the Senate Historical Office (2015).

59. Jeffries (2001, 535–44); Segal and Epstein (2005, 39); Ward (2003, 197–200).
60. Ibid. Stewart is here referring to Plato's *Republic* (5.473c–d).
61. Segal and Epstein (2005, 39); Ward (2003, 194).
62. Refer to footnote 20 in the O'Connor case study.

BIBLIOGRAPHY

Bailey, Michael A. *Measuring Court Preferences, 1950–2011: Agendas, Polarity and Heterogeneity*, 1–37. Department of Government and Public Policy Institute: Georgetown University, 2012.

Baker, Peter, and Jeff Zeleny. "Souter's Exit to Give Obama First Opening." *The New York Times Company*. May 1, 2009. http://www.nytimes.com/2009/05/02/us/02souter.html.

Clark, Tom S. "Measuring Ideological Polarization on the United States Supreme Court." *Political Research Quarterly* (2009): 146–57.

Federal Judicial Center. The Judiciary Act of 1801: "An Act to Provide for the More Convenient Organization of the Courts of the United States." *Federal Judicial Center*, February 13, 1801. http://www.fjc.gov/history/home.nsf/page/landmark_03.html.

Garrow, David J. "Mental Decrepitude on the U.S. Supreme Court: The Historical Case for a 28th Amendment." *The University of Chicago Law Review* 67, 4 (2000): 995–1087.

Gustman, Alan L., and Thomas L. Steinmeier. "A Structural Retirement Model." *Econometrica* 54 (1986): 555–84.

Ho, Daniel E., and Kevin M. Quinn. "How Not to Lie with Judicial Votes: Misconceptions, Measurement, and Models." *California Law Review* 98, 3 (2010): 813–76.

Kuhn, David Paul. "The Incredible Polarization and Politicization of the Supreme Court." *The Atlantic*, June 29, 2012. http://www.theatlantic.com/politics/archive/2012/06/the-incredible-polarization-and-politicization-of-the-supreme-court/259155/.

Obermayer, Herman. *States, Rehnquist: A Personal Portrait of the Distinguished Chief Justice of the United*. New York: Threshold Editions, 2009.

Peppers, Todd C., and M. Chad Oldfather. "Till Death Do Us Part: Chief Justices and the United States Supreme Court." *Marquette Law Review* 95, 2 (2011): 709–33.

Prakash, Saikrishna. "America's Aristocracy." *Yale Law Journal* 109 (1999): 580.

Segal, Jeffrey A., and Albert D. Cover. "Ideological Values and the Votes of U.S. Supreme Court Justices." *The American Political Science Review* 83, 2 (1989): 557–65.

Squire, Peverill. "Politics and Personal Factors in Retirement from the United States Supreme Court." *Political Behavior* 10, 2 (1988): 180–90.

Stock, James H., and David A. Wise. 1990. "Pensions, the Option Value of Work, and Retirement." *Econometrica* 58 (1980): 1151–80.

The Supreme Court Historical Society. n.d. Timeline of the Justices. The Supreme Court Historical Society. http://supremecourthistory.org/history_timeline.html.

Ward, Artemus. *Deciding to Leave: The Politics of Retirement from the United States Supreme Court*. Albany: State University of New York Press, 2003.

Wermiel, Stephen. "Changes on High Court are Likely to Increase Conservatives' Clout." *Wall Street Journal*, June 18, 1986.

Wikipedia Contributors. List of Justices of the Supreme Court of the United States. Wikipedia, The Free Encyclopedia, 2015. https://en.wikipedia.org/wiki/List_of_Justices_of_the_Supreme_Court_of_the_United_States#List_of_justices.

Woodruff, Adam Bonica and Michael J. "A Common-Space Measure of State Supreme Court Ideology." *Journal of Law, Economics, & Organization* (2014): 34–45. http://web.stanford.edu/~bonica/files/BW_ssc_ideology.pdf.

Zorn, Christopher J. W., and Steven R. Van Winkle. "A Competing Risks Model of Supreme Court Vacancies, 1789–1992." *Political Behavior* 22, 2 (2000): 145–66.

Conclusion

Drawing Conclusions about the Politicization of the Court

The politicization of the Court can originate from multiple sources. We began by elucidating two dominant models of juridical philosophy—the Legalist and Attitudinal models—and their effects on their adherents in terms of how those adherents tend to understand the law. Legalist judges tended to be more conservative with respect to the political climate of their nation and were considerably more cognizant and reverent of the history of the philosophy of law. Contrarily, Attitudinally oriented judges tended to be more forward thinking and progressive; they tended to identify more closely with what was considered liberal in their nation and thought about how best they could understand the Constitution in a way that promoted values of a more modern and enlightened world. Although these differing ideologies are philosophically incompatible, they represent juridical perspectives that, in some way or another, exemplify the two needs of a commonwealth. The Legalist model, with its endorsement of and reverence for precedent, tradition, and strict adherence to the text of law, secures the wisdom of experience that has accrued over the many centuries since the origin of Western law in Rome. Meanwhile, the Attitudinalist model properly comprehends a fundamental aim of legal philosophy to be that which aims at the good of man, as John Stuart Mill put it, "as a *progressive* being."[1] This model takes into account the need of humanity to evolve past traditions founded in and constituted by ignorance and vice. Although each draws the ire of political parties which reject their respective fundamental theses, they are integral to a body of law which can adapt alongside a changing world while at the same time not sacrificing its stalwartness or consistency.

Another source of the politicization of the Court arises from the process of the nomination of Supreme Court Justices. Due to the fact that the sitting

President has an incentive to perpetuate his legacy and support his party, and because a similar incentive applies collectively to the Senate, justices will often be preferred or ill-favored on the basis of political affiliation, rather than their explicit qualifications as a legal expert. As a result of this partisan disposition in government, it is more likely that judges associated with liberal values will be successfully nominated when they are younger and less qualified, whereas conservative judges must be relatively older and more experienced for their nominations to be as successful. Moreover, judges who are more liberal also face less arduous and lengthy confirmation periods, while the opposite is true for conservative judges. This can often be laid at the feet of the Senate which has, in the period under investigation, been under Democrat control for a greater period of time than it has been under Republican control.

The diminishing docket was another area that we chose to focus our attention, and we specifically made note of the fact that differing ideological views can be responsible for how many cases a Court will tend to hear. More conservative Courts are more likely than liberal ones to hear fewer cases, and the number of cases likely to reach the Supreme Court diminishes as tensions rise during periods in which the president's party affiliation is at odds with those of the majority of the Senate.

One area of surprise from our work on this text was to find that retirements of the Court were significantly less politicized than one would suspect at first glance. Although retirements from the Court provide ample opportunities for political bias to enter the affairs of the Court, just less than half of the justices who have retired in recent years have done so without being strategic in terms of who their replacement might be. For a judge, being able to retire during the term of a president of the same party would seem to be a political boon for both the president in terms of their legacy, and the judge in terms of the sorts of judgments they would like to see come from the Court. Moreover, the justice could just as easily hang on for dear life in old age to a Court that is passing through a period of time when a president of an opposing ideology is serving, and hope that, next election, they are replaced by someone with a congruent ideology. Thus, while the process is certainly politicized, it is politicized to a lesser extent than some of the other areas concerning the politicization of the Court.

TO THE READER

Although this book is not intended to be a normative guide, or to move one to accept a particular viewpoint or other—it is rather to demonstrate that the court is a politicized entity—it is prudent, we think, to end on a normative note.

It is not uncommon for the Court to be politicized, nor it is uncommon for the Court to politicize itself; our work here shows at least this much. However, this politicization ought to be abhorred. The politicization of the Court, either by members of other branches of the federal government, or by the justices themselves in ruling, not strictly in accordance with a reasoned legal philosophy, but in accordance with their own political biases, should only be as a bastardization of its essential purpose and function. The Court does not exist as an extension of the legislative branch, nor does it serve a wing of the executive which can strike down laws from a legislature controlled by ideological opponents. It cannot be intended as anything other than the third and final check and balance upon the other two branches of government. It is as Montesquieu claimed

> Again, there is no liberty, if the power of judging be not separated from the legislative and executive powers. Were it joined with the legislative, the life and liberty of the subject would be exposed to arbitrary control, for the judge would then be the legislator. Were it joined to the executive power, the judge might behave with all the violence of an oppressor.[2]

The judges of the Supreme Court are to be, according to Alexander Hamilton, "faithful guardians of the Constitution."[3] While many have complained about the method and means of this guardianship, particularly about judicial review,[4] the intention of the Founders is clear: if the Supreme Court did not have judicial review, it wouldn't be a proper check and balance on either the executive or the legislative branches of government. It would therefore fail in its fundamental institutional task. Yes, while the Court's primary function as the judiciary branch is to be the highest and final appellate Court in the land, its primary function in the greater context of the government of the United States is to serve as a check and balance against the other two branches. To this end, the legislature and the executive suffer themselves to be judged by the Court in all matters, save those in which it is the Constitution itself being amended. Referring to Hamilton again

> A Constitution is, in fact, and must be regarded by the judges as, a fundamental law. It therefore belongs to them to ascertain its meaning, as well as the meaning of any particular act proceeding from the legislative body. If there should happen to be an irreconcilable variance between the two, that which has the superior obligation and validity ought, of course, to be preferred; or, in other words, the Constitution ought to be preferred to the statute.[5]

Is it not clear that this is what it means to be a guardian of the Constitution, and therefore the spirit of the laws and of the people? The Court is the institution that binds the executive and the legislative branches *to* the

Constitution; they suffer themselves to be judged by the Court should they act unconstitutionally.

As such, if you are someone with reverence for the American Founders and their wisdom, or someone who possesses a deep faith in the purposes of a commonwealth, the rule of law, and in justice, then take into consideration the politicization of the Supreme Court that surrounds us every day. Often, especially during election seasons, you will hear prospective candidates for president chastise the Supreme Court for a particular decision, or deride the "slant" of the Court as yet another instance of party bias which is incongruous to that politician's own. Soon after, they will declare their intentions to nominate a justice who shares *their* values. Not a justice who is supremely qualified as a constitutional scholar and who has mastered the legal-philosophical art no. This is unimportant to that politician if that judge were to rule in a way that was contrary to the expected outcomes of the politician. If the trait most worth advertising about a prospective judicial nominee is "they will rule as I wish them to rule," then that nominee is a failure and will not accord with the foundational ends of the Court and the Nation itself. Anyone who professes such goals and exudes such rhetoric is worthy of suspicion insofar as they claim to be a servant of the people. If you are an American reader—or even someone who is considering coming to this Nation—then we implore you to understand that this scrupulousness is a necessary part of the constitution of a good citizen.

Recently, a well-respected judge, Judge Richard Posner, who serves on the United States Court of Appeals for the Seventh Circuit in Chicago, has made controversial remarks about the Constitution. Posner wrote that

> I see absolutely no value to a judge of spending decades, years, months, weeks, day, hours, minutes, or seconds studying the Constitution, the history of its enactment, its amendments, and its implementation (across the centuries—well, just a little more than two centuries, and of course less for many of the amendments). Eighteenth-century guys, however smart, could not foresee the culture, technology, etc., of the 21st century. Which means that the original Constitution, the Bill of Rights, and the post–Civil War amendments (including the 14th), do not speak to today. David Strauss is right: The Supreme Court treats the Constitution like it is authorizing the court to create a common law of constitutional law, based on current concerns, not what those 18th century guys were worrying about. In short, let's not let the dead bury the living.[6]

Although Posner is not a Supreme Court Justice, it seems as though Hamilton's maxim that justices be "faithful guardians of the Constitution" ought to be taken as a maxim for *any* judge. A judge's comments that repudiate such founding sentiments are such that they are undermining of the very legitimacy of such a judge's tenure on any court in the United States—a somewhat ironical consequence of Posner's remarks. Due to the controversial nature of Posner's comments, he has since walked back those remarks, stating that those remarks were not clearly stated, and that what he was primarily getting at was that certain provisions of the Constitution were purposely vague in order to facilitate compromise among the delegates of the several states at the time of its adoption. He did not retract his remarks about the Founder's being "18th century guys," stating that "the framers of the Constitution were very intelligent and experienced, but they could no more foresee conditions in the 21st century than we can foresee conditions in the 23rd century."[7] One hopes that Posner sees the irony in lacking clarity in one's criticism of something for its purported vagueness.

Posner's original sentiment is increasingly commonplace as more progressive political movements gain strength. Traditional wisdom is discarded under the mistaken notion that whatever is too old (how old is too old to be progressive, anyway?) is irrelevant to our concerns today. This is the same sort of thinking that would close a mind to reading Plato, Aquinas, Confucius, or Locke because, after all: what could a bunch of ancients who predated all, or most of, modern science possibly have to contribute to the human condition today? It is the mistaken notion that we today are better, smarter, and wiser than any generation that has preceded us; this is a notion which is properly analogous to the hubris of youth and the dismissal of parental guidance. It is a supreme sort of arrogance to think oneself as wiser than Aristotle or Kant simply because your existence is temporally posterior to theirs, or because you have access to empirical facts about the world that remained unknown to them, as though that constitutes wisdom in the first place. Remarks of this sort are unbecoming of a Constitutional scholar like Posner and are worrisome coming from average citizens, as they constitute a repudiation of the wise by the unwise; a repudiation of wisdom by ignorance.

THE CURRENT STATE OF THE COURT

Since Antonin Scalia died in early 2016, the Court has been an ideological talking point—especially during the 2016 election cycle. Pundits and ideologues speculated about the fate of the Court by considering what kinds of legislation, repudiated or mandated by the Court, might be in the country's future. The vacancy on the Court could serve as an important political pivot; it would simultaneously afford a president indirect control over the legislative future of the nation at the same time that it would preserve their legacy, assuming, of course, they selected a Justice who saw and interpreted the law as they do. Although the presidential candidates made this subject a big talking point for their campaigns, promising to appoint justices that would work from the bench in the favor of their stated ideological and political goals, President Obama had the first shot at filling this vacancy and securing an aspect of his presidential legacy.

In an attempt to fill the hole left by Justice Scalia on the Court, President Obama nominated Merrick Garland, who was and is currently a judge on the United States Court of Appeals for the District of Columbia. Garland was a rather moderate, left-leaning judge—not the sort that then presidential candidate Clinton would have preferred, given her statements about potential nominations made on the campaign trail—and so was perhaps seen by President Obama as being less disagreeable than other potential Justices. President Obama, however, faced extremely heavy and unrelenting opposition in his nomination of Garland from the Senate. The Senate, which was controlled by a Republican majority at the time that President Obama announced his nominee, refused to consider a vote on the nomination. Garland's nomination, while the subject of quite a bit of controversy, eventually expired at the end of the 114th Congress.

Advice and Consent, the process through which the Senate of the United States votes and approves the president's nominee, is another element comprising the totality of the institution of the Court (given that it selects the Justices), and unsurprisingly, as was the case in 2016, it has become increasingly and explicitly politicized. The actions of the Senate in 2016 were not entirely unprecedented. While many pundits and politicians complained of the Republican stonewalling of President Obama's attempts to refill the Bench, video surfaced indicating that this tactic was rather bipartisan; in 1992, Joe Biden, then a senator, argued that

> I am sure, Mr. President, after having uttered these words some will criticize such a decision and say it was nothing more than an attempt to save the seat on the Court in the hopes that a Democrat will be permitted to fill it, but that would not be our intention, Mr. President, if that were the course to choose in the Senate to not consider holding hearings until after the election. Instead, it would be our pragmatic conclusion that once the political season is under way, and it is, action on a Supreme Court nomination must be put off until after the election campaign is over. That is what is fair to the nominee and is central to the process. Otherwise, it seems to me, Mr. President, we will be in deep trouble as an institution.[8]

Yet, when the republicans did something quite similar in 2016, Joe Biden claimed that "we're setting an incredibly dangerous precedent in the institution that I love, that I served in 36 years."[9] It is not surprising that politicians choose to exploit political institutions for their own gain when it suits them, whilst condemning their political opponents from doing the same. Yet it is worrisome that *yet another* aspect of the Court—the nomination process specifically—the branch intended to be the most politically neutral, faces politicization, and faces it at seemingly every turn. While it is the Senate's place to offer its advice and consent in conjunction with a presidential nomination, the doctrine of Advice and Consent does not provide the Senate with a *license* to entirely dictate the terms of the nomination process. Advice and Consent is yet another product of the wisdom of the founders, through which they have once again set the branches of the federal government against one another by involving both the legislators and the executors. This indicates that Advice and Consent not only aims to satisfy the function purpose of the tripartite structure of government inspired by Montesquieu, but also that it was considered integral to the common good of the nation, the very thing the Senate is charged with promoting and safeguarding; a functional Court is a necessity in a nation which respects and honors the rule and historical legacy of the law. As platitudinous as it might sound to say or to read, this politicization for political gains has no business interfering or intermingling with this duty to the common good.

Neil Gorsuch, who was confirmed by the Senate in April of 2017, also faced his share of this politicization, as Senate Democrats led a filibuster against him, withholding from Gorsuch the traditionally necessary 60 votes needed to secure a successful nomination. The filibuster was not cut entirely along ideological lines, as several Democratic Senators voted in favor of judge Gorsuch, but it still reflected a broad political divide between the two parties in the Senate, which some speculate is due to continued opposition to President Trump.[10] The Senate Republicans, not to be out-politicized, invoked the so-called "nuclear option" which allows the traditionally necessary 60 votes needed to the Senate to confirm a Supreme Court nominee to be reduced to a mere simple majority—51 votes.[11] It stands to reason that, if this process were not politicized, a nominee with Gorsuch's record—a lettered legal education, tenure on the Court of Appeals, and his formal academic qualifications (a PhD as a legal and moral philosopher)—would not draw such clear partisan divide and the employment of tactics to secure a political victory, rather than a victory for the commonwealth in electing in eminently qualified legal scholar to the Court.

President Trump would seem to have made good on his promise to select a nominee "in the mold of [Antonin] Scalia" as Gorsuch, though perhaps with some important caveats, claims to be an originalist, thereby sharing the same legal philosophy as the late Justice Scalia. One important caveat to whatever idiosyncratic understanding of originalism is likely to be Gorsuch's *moral* philosophy; Gorsuch adheres to the moral philosophy of natural law theory, which he likely inherited from a conjunction of his Catholic background and his dissertation supervisor and mentor, the legal philosopher John Finnis, who is one of the foremost natural law theorists alive today.[12] While Gorsuch and Scalia may not adhere to an identical legal philosophy (though Scalia was himself a Catholic), the natural law view of morality is usually engendered by political and moral conservatism, and *this* would be in the spirit—or mold—of Antonin Scalia. Gorsuch's nomination and confirmation set a precedent which is both interesting and encouraging. This appears to be the first time in the history of the court that that a formally qualified moral and legal philosopher—trained at one of the most respected departments of philosophy, no less—has sat on the bench. It will be interesting to watch this Court unfold, and to witness the ways in which Justice Gorsuch brings his moral and legal philosophical training to bear on his work on the Court.

FINAL WORDS

If there is anything that we hope you take from this work, it is an appreciation of the Supreme Court as an institution and a healthy skepticism concerning its neutrality in matters of politics. Although the Court was designed to be isolated, in part, from political matters, the disease of partisan strife entered into the institution almost as soon as there was a Court to infiltrate. This is not to say that such a thing is permanent or irrevocable—but it is to say that it is here with us now. Something that it is important to recognize is that the Court is inextricably tied, through the nomination process and the Senate confirmation process, to the other two branches of government. Therefore, it stands to reason that increases partisan divisions in those branches of government will bleed into divisions in terms of the distribution of judges on the bench, and subsequently, into the decisions those justices eventually will hand down. Although the politicization of the Court has developed for many decades—even longer many would argue—this does not change how we as citizens ought to respond.

Consider in this recent election what we have seen from some of the frontrunners of the presidential race. Hillary Clinton, for example, in her 2016 bid for the presidency claimed to have a litmus test for prospective Court nominees. Judges who would oppose ruling like *Citizens United* and who would support *Roe v. Wade* and marriage equality are those who would pass Clinton's test. Each one of these tests is centered on contested, partisan divides—and Clinton would desire a judge who sees eye to eye with her on these matters. Purpose oriented qualifications are apparently not worth mentioning.[13] Ted Cruz, another prospective candidate for president in 2016 offered potential voters something similar, saying that "Over and over again we keep electing Republican presidents for whom the court is not a priority." . . . "I give you my solemn word, every justice that I put on the court will be a principled constitutionalist who will be faithful to the law and will not legislate from the bench."[14] These seemingly contradictory statements—republicans making the Court a strategic ideological goal and vowing to appoint justices who do not legislate from the bench—represent this partisanship from the other side of isle. Even Vermont Senator Bernie Sanders sees the Court as a political tool to utilize in shaping policy, claiming that any justice he would nominate would be committed to overturning the *Citizens United* decision.[15] While it is certainly the case that many legal experts might back any of these candidates up in terms of their views about particular cases, what is striking is that, when prompted to speak about matters of the nomination of jurists to the Court, or when they make it a point to speak about it, what is primary for them is the ideology of the justice and what they can do in terms of advancing policy.

Only time will tell when it comes to the future politicization or depoliticization of the Court in coming years; one can hope that the institution will find its way, along with the other branches of government, back to those foundational principles which legitimized them. Although this is an unlikely result of things to come, it does not change the emphasis that every citizen ought to have on depoliticizing the Court. We hope that you share this concern with us, and move forward as a more informed citizen.

NOTES

1. *On Liberty*, Ch. I, Pg. 19.
2. Baron de Montesquieu, *The Spirit of the Laws*, XI.VI.
3. *Federalist 78.*
4. "Judicial review is the idea, fundamental to the U.S. system of government, that the actions of the executive and legislative branches of government are subject to review and possible invalidation by the judicial branch. Judicial review allows the Supreme Court to take an active role in ensuring that the other branches of government abide by the constitution" (Cornell University Law School, n.d.).
5. *Federalist 78.*
6. See Posner (2016b).
7. See Posner (2016a).
8. See Biden (1992).
9. See McCaskill (2016).
10. See Flegenheimer (2017).
11. See Killough and Barrett (2017).
12. You can read more about this philosophy in Kelleher (2017).
13. See Easley (2016).
14. See Lithwick (2016).
15. See Bradner (2015).

BIBLIOGRAPHY

Biden, Joe. 1992. https://www.realclearpolitics.com/video/2016/02/22/biden_in_1992_bush_should_not_name_a_nominee_until_after_the_november_election.html.

Bradner, Eric. "Bernie Sanders Has a Supreme Court Litmus Test." *CNN*, May 10, 2015. http://www.cnn.com/2015/05/10/politics/bernie-sanders-supreme-court-litmus-test-election-2016/.

Cornell University Law School. *Judicial Review*. Cornell University. n.d. https://www.law.cornell.edu/wex/judicial_review.

Easley, Jonathan. "Clinton: 'I have a bunch of litmus tests' for Supreme Court Nominees." Capitol Hill Publishing Corp. February 3, 2016. http://thehill.com/blogs/ballot-box/presidential-races/268174-clinton-i-have-a-bunch-of-litmus-tests-for-supreme-court.

Flegenheimer, Matt. "Senate Republicans Deploy 'Nuclear Option' to Clear Path for Gorsuch." April 6, 2017. https://www.nytimes.com/2017/04/06/us/politics/neil-gorsuch-supreme-court-senate.html.

Kelleher, J. Paul. "Neil Gorsuch's 'natural law' Philosophy Is a Long Way From Justice Scalia's Originalism." March 20, 2017. https://www.vox.com/the-big-idea/2017/3/20/14976926/gorsuch-natural-law-supreme-court-hearings.

Killough, Ashley, and Ted Barrett. "Senate GOP Triggers Nuclear Option to Break Democratic Filibuster on Gorsuch." April 7, 2017. http://www.cnn.com/2017/04/06/politics/senate-nuclear-option-neil-gorsuch/index.html.

Lithwick, Dahlia. "Ted Cruz Won't Prevent the Next John Roberts." The Slate Group LLC. February 9, 2016.

McCaskill, Nolan D. "Biden Urges Senate GOP to Hold Garland Vote." September 8, 2016. http://www.politico.com/story/2016/09/joe-biden-senate-merrick-garland-227894.

Posner, Richard. "Supreme Court Breakfast Table – Entry 27: Broad Interpretations." The Slate Group LLC. July 1, 2016. http://www.slate.com/articles/news_and_politics/the_breakfast_table/features/2016/supreme_court_breakfast_table_for_june_2016/richard_posner_clarifies_his_views_on_the_constitution.html (accessed July 24, 2016).

———. "Supreme Court Breakfast Table – Entry 9: The Academy Is Out of Its Depth." The Slate Group LLC. June 24, 2016. http://www.slate.com/articles/news_and_politics/the_breakfast_table/features/2016/supreme_court_breakfast_table_for_june_2016/law_school_professors_need_more_practical_experience.html (accessed July 24, 2016).

Index

Note: Page numbers in italics refers to figure and table

About the Authors

Justin P. DePlato, PhD, is associate professor of political science at Robert Morris University. He is the author of several books on the U.S. presidency including *The Cavalier Presidency: Executive Power and Prerogative in Times of Crisis* and *American Democracy: American Founders, Presidents and Enlightened Philosophers*.

Matthew Markulin, research assistant, is a law student at the University of Pittsburgh studying tax law.

www.ingramcontent.com/pod-product-compliance
Ingram Content Group UK Ltd.
Pitfield, Milton Keynes, MK11 3LW, UK
UKHW041122071026
15587UKWH00009B/72

9 781498 512183